KNIT YOUR HEART OUT

Over 30 ways to knit a heart
for someone special

Bente Presterud Røvik

KNIT YOUR HEART OUT

Over 30 ways to knit a heart
for someone special

David and Charles

www.stitchcraftcreate.co.uk

Contents

Introduction

When I started this book, I thought to myself, I like hearts; but then who doesn't?

AND THEN I LET MYSELF GET CARRIED AWAY…

…by the endless possibilities, and by the shapes and colors…. So I allowed myself to play around. I made hearts in single and multiple colors, with and without patterns, plainly knitted or with texture. Some hearts were turned inside out, others were put upside down, some were hung up on string or attached to a wreath. Most are knitted in yarn, but some are made in paper and metal. Some hearts have become birds that can't fly, pieces of jewelry, and trays filled with popcorn. There are 127 unique hearts in this book – and there could have been many more!

HEART'S CHOICE

There is one heart that I particularly liked. I also asked my boys and some of the contributors to this book if they had favorite hearts too. Everybody chose one, and none of us chose the same one. You can learn each person's thoughts on their favorite hearts throughout the book.

DESIGN YOUR OWN HEART

It's easy to do! I've included a workshop on this at the end of the book (see p. 118). You can decide on the yarn type, colors, and pattern, and then follow the instructions to make your own heart!

IF YOU DON'T KNOW HOW TO KNIT

…try looking at Bente's little knitting class (see pp. 120–123) to get started.

THANK YOU!

Making a book is fun, but also a lot of work. I had good helpers along the way.

A warm thank you to Anne Britt! Together we knitted all of the hearts in this book – me one half and her the other half. Loyal and determined, she knitted her way through, stitch by stitch, heart by heart. There ended up being a lot of hearts! Many thanks to Inger Margrethe, who picked just the right superwoman to design this book.
Photographer Guri, stylist Alexandra, and Laila on layout – you did an excellent job. I am very pleased!
A heartfelt thank you to my boys at home, who put up with my creative mess, my mental absence, and my occasional bad moods – I'm not going to deny that making a book has its stressful periods.
And, of course, a gigantic thanks to the boss up there, who created creativity, and gave us hearts.

Let's use them warmly!

Bente

www.benterovik.no

7

ALL THE HEARTS IN THIS BOOK ARE KNITTED USING THE SAME BASIC PATTERN. YOU CAN KNIT THEM IN TWO DIFFERENT SIZES: **REGULAR** OR **LONG.**

WHAT KIND OF NEEDLES DO YOU USE?

CIRCULAR NEEDLES OR DOUBLE-POINTED NEEDLES?

The hearts are knitted in the round. Most people will probably find it more natural to use short double-pointed needles and then change to a circular needle if the heart is big enough to allow this.

Alternatively, you could use two circular needles for the smaller hearts. For example, you could have the front-piece stitches on one needle and the back-piece stitches on the other. When knitting the front piece, use the front-piece needle and when knitting the back piece, use the back-piece needle.

Do whatever works best for you!

WHAT SIZE NEEDLES DO YOU USE?

You should use knitting needles suitable to the weight of the yarn, and that give a slightly tight gauge so the heart is not loosely knitted or see-through (unless that's the purpose, of course).

Each pattern has a suggested needle size, but the gauge is more important than the specific size of the needle.

STARTING OUT

The beginning of the heart can be a bit of a challenge!

You will have just a few stitches on the round, and if you are using small double-pointed needles some of the stitches can easily fall off.

It's a good idea to use only three needles at the beginning: Put the front-piece stitches on one of the needles; put the back-piece stitches on the second, and use the third one to knit. Use more needles later when it's more practical.

GAUGE

Follow the gauge in order to achieve the measurements listed in the pattern instructions. Each pattern suggests the needle size, but there is no guarantee you will achieve this gauge when you knit. If you tend to knit tightly, you might have to use larger needles than suggested to achieve the correct gauge; if you knit loosely, you might have to use smaller needles. That being said, it won't usually matter if your heart ends up a different size from the ones seen in this book!

Make sure you don't knit too loosely, especially when making a heart that is intended to be stuffed. It is better to have a dense fabric so you can't see the wadding inside and so the wadding doesn't poke out through loose stitches.

Also remember that if you have a different gauge, the amount of yarn you use might change slightly – you may need a bit more or a little less yarn than the amount suggested.

WADDING

The hearts can be made with or without wadding. If you do want to stuff a heart, wadding is the most obvious option. You can buy this at most craft stores. I bought some pillows and used the wadding from them – an easy and cheap alternative. You could also stuff the heart with other materials, such as yarn leftovers (in small hearts) or beanbag filling.

YARN

Knit your heart in cotton, wool, or synthetic fibers, or use metal, paper, or plastic thread. Try thin, thick, or many threads … Experiment and try out different types of yarn, exciting combinations, and fun embellishments.

REUSE

Use whatever leftovers you have, both for yarn and embellishments. If the yarn is relatively fine, you won't need much to make a heart. The smallest hearts in this book require only 5oz (1.5g) of yarn.

If you have only small amounts of yarn in different colors, try knitting stripes or a color pattern. If you have some chunky and some fine yarns, you can use one strand of chunky and several strands of fine yarn together.

Decorate the hearts with buttons, silk flowers, leftover beads and ribbons – you name it! I often use whatever I have lying around. I first make a small pile of the yarn and material I would like to use, then add some and remove some until I'm happy. There is no guarantee of a great result, but it's a good start.

BASIC HEART PATTERN

Size: Regular[Long].

NOTE: Read the instructions for the whole pattern before you start.

INCREASE TIP: Make an increase by lifting up the thread between 2 sts and twisting it before placing it on the right-hand needle, then knit this twisted stitch.

Knit the whole heart in st st unless otherwise instructed.

BASE OF THE HEART: Cast on 5 sts and join to work in the round. (This will be fiddly when there are only a few sts, so try dividing the sts over two double-pointed needles and knitting with a third until there are enough stitches to divide over three needles and knit with a fourth.) K one round. Inc to 10 sts on next round. Place a marker at beg of the round, and a marker in the middle of the round. (5 sts at the front and 5 sts at the back of the heart.) Work in st st around. At the same time, work every 3rd[4th] round like this: *K1, inc1, k to 1 st before marker, inc1, k1*, knit from * to * one more time. (4 sts increased on the round.) Rep the incs until you have 46 sts. After the last inc, knit a further 2[3] rounds. On the next round, inc 1 st in the middle st in the front and 1 st in the middle st at the back – work the inc by knitting into the front and back of the same stitch. (48 sts.)

Next round: K12, put the next 24 sts on a stitch holder, cast on 2 sts (these cast-on sts will be in the lowest dip of the curve), k to end of the round. (There are 26 sts to each of the heart curves.)

FIRST HEART CURVE: Place a marker at the beg of the round and a marker at the middle of the round. (13 sts to the front and 13 sts to the back of the curve.) You will cont working in the round, so divide the sts evenly over two needles and work with a third needle (this makes the work more manageable when there are fewer sts).

Rounds 1–5: Even.

Round 6: *K1, k2tog, k until 3 sts rem before the marker, sl1 kwise, k1, psso, k1*, knit from * to * one more time. (22 sts.)

Rounds 7–8: Even.

Round 9: K as for row 6. (18 sts.)

Round 10: Even.

Round 11: K as for row 6. (14 sts.)

Round 12: *K2tog, bind off 3 sts, sl1 kwise, k1, psso, bind off 1 st*, k from * to * one more time.

Tie off the yarn and cut, leaving a long enough yarn end to sew up the gap. Lay the heart flat and stitch together the gap at the top of the curve of the heart. You may find it easier to part-fill the heart with wadding at this stage, as there will only be a small gap left at the end.

SECOND HEART CURVE: Removing the rem 24 sts from the holder, place 12 sts on one needle for the back half and 12 sts on another needle for the front half. Attach the working yarn at the side edge of the heart, k12 sts for back, cast on 2 sts (these will be in the dip of the curve), and k12 sts for front. Then work rounds 1–12 as for the first heart curve.

TO FINISH: Sew together the opening at the bottom of the heart. Fill the rest of the heart with wadding, and then sew together the remaining gap in the center. Weave in any yarn ends.

YOU CAN ALTER THE SIZE OF THE HEART BY VARYING THE THICKNESS OF THE YARN AND SIZE OF THE NEEDLES. USING FINE YARN AND SMALL NEEDLES WILL MAKE A SMALL HEART. USING THICK YARN AND BIG NEEDLES WILL MAKE LARGER HEARTS.

MAKING DIFFERENT SIZE HEARTS

SMALL HEART CUSHION

HEART MEASUREMENTS: Width 9½in (24cm), height 11½in (29cm).

MATERIALS:
• Wadding

YARN: Dale Condor (50% alpaca, 50% wool, 100g = 142yd/130m), 100g off-white 0010.

NEEDLES: US 8 (5mm).

GAUGE: 10 sts x 15 rows with yarn held double = 4 x 4in (10 x 10cm).

Cast on with the yarn held double, and knit the Regular heart (see p. 9). Turn the finished piece inside out, stuff with wadding, and sew up the gaps.

♥ ———————————————————

LARGE HEART CUSHION

HEART MEASUREMENTS: Width 17in (43.5cm), height 21¼in (54cm).

MATERIALS:
• Wadding

YARN: Dale Condor (50% alpaca, 50% wool, 100g = 142yd/130m), 600g black/off white 0090.

NEEDLES: US 19 (15mm).

GAUGE: 5.5 sts x 8 rows with six strands of yarn held together = 4 x 4in (10 x 10cm).

Cast on with six strands of yarn held together and knit the Regular heart (see p. 9). Turn the finished piece inside out, stuff with wadding, and sew up the gaps.

♥ ———————————————————

MEDIUM HEART CUSHION

HEART MEASUREMENTS: Width 13½in (34.5cm), height 17in (43cm).

MATERIALS:
• Wadding

YARN: Dale Condor (50% alpaca, 50% wool, 100g = 142yd/130m), 300g light charcoal/off white 0083.

NEEDLES: US 15 (10mm).

GAUGE: 7 sts x 10 rows with four strands of yarn held together = 4 x 4in (10 x 10cm).

Cast on with four strands of yarn held together and knit the Regular heart (see p. 9). Turn the finished piece inside out, stuff with wadding, and sew up the gaps.

Tip

When you are knitting with two strands of yarn held together but only have one ball of yarn, take the end of the yarn from the middle of the ball and knit it together with the end of the yarn on the outside of the ball.

The white heart is knitted with two strands of yarn held together, the gray and white with four, and the black and white with six. The result is small, medium, and large cushions.

gresslok

Everyday hearts

Persille

KNITTING THIS HEART TOOK SOME EFFORT, BUT
WHEN IT WAS FINISHED I THOUGHT IT WAS WORTH
EVERY SINGLE ONE OF THE 1,472 STITCHES!

HEART TRAY

PAPER YARN TRAY

HEART MEASUREMENTS: Width 15¾in (40cm),
height 19in (48cm).

MATERIALS:
- Paper yarn assortment
- A large round balloon
- Wallpaper paste
- Small paintbrush
- 98in (2.5m) of thick metal wire
- Adhesive (for example, a glue gun)

NEEDLES: US 19 (15mm).

GAUGE: 6 sts x 9 rows with six strands of yarn held
together = 4 x 4in (10 x 10cm).

♥ ─────────────────────────────

HEART: Cast on one strand of the paper
yarn in each of light green, green,
turquoise, blue, yellow, and pink (six
strands of yarn held together), and knit the
Regular heart (see p. 9).

SUPPORT: Blow up the balloon and place
it somewhere you can hold it steady (for
example, in a cardboard box a little smaller
than the balloon). Apply plenty of adhesive
on both sides of the heart and place it over
the balloon to give the tray a curved shape.
Leave to dry – this can take some time (up
to several days).

Apply additional layers of adhesive to
obtain a stiffer or firmer tray, if you wish.

LEGS: Cut six lengths of metal wire
measuring 15¾in (40cm) each. Fold each
piece double. Place two pieces in a cross
shape and wrap the paper yarn (in the
desired color) tightly around the cross.
Then bend all the arms in the cross slightly
upward, so the middle of the cross becomes
the point of one leg. Bend the end of each
arm outward so they lay flat against the
underside of the tray (see picture below).

Make three legs like this and attach them to
the underneath of the tray using a glue gun.

 The colors of the tray will
become slightly lighter for
each layer of adhesive applied.
Apply the extra layers of
adhesive on the underside of
the tray if you wish to retain
the brightness of the colors.

*The tray has three legs.
These have a core of metal
wire. Shape the wire into a
cross and wind paper yarn
around before it is glued to
the underside of the tray.*

The tray is made out of paper yarn. The finished tray is soaked in adhesive before being placed on a balloon to achieve the desired curved shape.

WHAT'S INSIDE THE HEART...

SCENTED HEARTS

HEART MEASUREMENTS: Width 4½in (11.5cm),
height 6¼in (16cm).

MATERIALS:

- Wadding
- Small silk flowers and/or leaves
- Ribbon or string for hanging loops
- Pot pourri

YARN: Pandora (100% cotton, 50g = 195yd/180m),
leftovers or 50g of each color listed by the chart for
each heart.

NEEDLES: US 6 (4mm), plus C2/D3 (3mm) crochet
hook to make the hanging loop (optional).

GAUGE: 21 sts x 27 rows in patt with the yarn held
double = 4 x 4in (10 x 10cm).

♥ —————————————————————————

HEART: Cast on with the yarn held double
using the color listed at the top of each
chart, and knit a Regular heart (see p. 9). At
the same time, after increasing to 10 sts, knit
the color patterns following the charts.

Fill the finished heart with wadding and pot
pourri, and sew up any gaps.

HANGING LOOP: Attach a piece of ribbon or
string to use as a hanging loop, or crochet
a loop (for the blue heart). Using a single
strand of blue yarn and size C2/D3 (3mm)
crochet hook, crochet a length of chain to
the desired length. Turn, and make 1 sl st in
each ch – make sure you don't make these
too tight.

EMBELLISHMENTS: Glue or sew on flowers
or leaves.

Tip

If you wish to replace the pot
pourri once in a while you can
attach a small popper or snap
fastener between the curves
of the heart, instead of sewing
it up. Cover it over with a flower
or other decoration.

Here I have chosen cute colors and decorations. If you want to create a different look, use other colors and replace the flowers with something that suits your style.

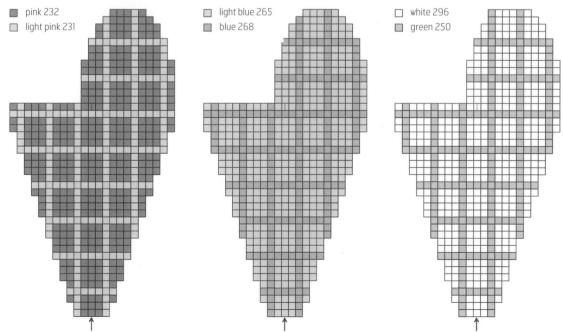

■ pink 232
□ light pink 231

□ light blue 265
■ blue 268

□ white 296
■ green 250

THESE STURDY PLANT LABELS WILL ADD SOME
FUN TO YOUR KITCHEN GARDEN – WHILE YOU
WAIT FOR THE VEGETABLES TO GROW!

HEART ON A STICK

GARDEN HEARTS

HEART MEASUREMENTS: Width 4in (10cm), height 4¾in (12cm).

MATERIALS:
- Wadding
- Wooden stakes with a diameter of ¼in (5–6mm)
- Green craft paint or waterproof felt-tip pen
- Cardboard

YARN: Petunia (100% cotton, 50g = 120yd/110m), 50g in each of yellow-green 216, green 217, and dark green 215; Pandora (100% cotton, 50g = 196yd/180m), leftovers or 50g in each of turquoise 267, cerise 251, and yellow-orange 204.

NEEDLES: US 4 (3.5mm), plus C2/D3 (3mm) and E4 (3.5mm) crochet hooks.

GAUGE: 24 sts x 36 rows = 4 x 4in (10 x 10cm).

CROCHET TOG TR (TREBLE CROCHET): Crochet each and every tr, but leave out the last. When you crochet the last tr, pull the yarn through all the loops on the hook.

♥ —————————————————————

CHIVE

HEART: Cast on with yellow-green yarn, and knit the Regular heart (see p. 9)

At the same time, after increasing to 10 sts, knit the color pattern following the chart.

Fill the finished heart with wadding and sew up any gaps.

FLOWER: Use yellow-orange yarn and C2/D3 (3mm) crochet hook.

Make 6 ch and join to form a circle with 1 sl st.

Crochet *3 ch + 2 crochet tog tr (see explanation left) + 3 ch + 1 sl st*, crochet from * to * a total of five times into the circle. (5 leaves.)

FLOWER CENTER: Use yellow-orange yarn and C2/D3 (3mm) crochet hook.

Crochet a bobble: Make a loose loop. Crochet 3 ch, then 4 crochet tog tr (see explanation left) in the loop. Cut the yarn. Tighten the loop and tie up the threads into a bobble.

☐ yellow-green 216
☐ green 217

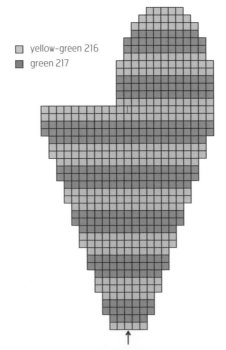

When the vegetable-growing season is over, remove the tags and use them as decoration somewhere else.

tomat

gresslok

LEAF: Use green yarn and size E4 (3.5mm) crochet hook. Crochet 9 ch. Make a turning ch of 2 ch and crochet like this in the 9 ch:

1 dc in first ch, 1 tr in next ch, 2 dtr in next ch, 1 dtr in each of the next 4 ch, 2 tr in next ch, then like this in the last st:

2 tr + 1 dtr + 1 picot (= 2 ch, crochet 1 sl st in the first of these) + 1 dtr + 2 tr.

Then cont along the other side of the foundation chain, with sts set like this:

2 dtr in next ch, 1 quad tr in each of the next 4 ch, 2 dtr in next ch, 1 tr in next ch, 1 dc in last ch, 1 sl st at the end of the leaf. Crochet another leaf.

TO FINISH: Sew the flower to the heart, and sew the bobble to the middle of the flower. Paint or color the wooden stake green and let it dry. Stick the stake through the heart. Glue or sew the leaves to the wooden pin. Cut a rectangle out of cardboard, then apply text and glue to the stake.

TOMATO

HEART: Cast on with yellow-green yarn, and knit Regular heart (see p. 9).

Fill the finished heart with wadding and sew together any gaps.

FLOWER: Use cerise yarn and size C2/D3 (3mm) crochet hook. Join 6 ch into a circle with 1 sl st.

Row 1: 5 ch (1 tr, 2 ch), *1 tr in the circle, 2 ch*, crochet from * to * a total of nine times, finishing with 1 sl st in 3rd ch at beg of row.

Row 2: Change to turquoise yarn. Crochet 1 sc + 3 ch + 1 tr + 3 ch + 1 sc in each of 2-ch.

FLOWER CENTER: Use yellow-orange yarn and C2/D3 (3mm) crochet hook.

Crochet a bobble: Make a loose loop. Crochet 3 ch, then 4 crochet tog tr (see p. 18) in the loop. Cut the thread, tighten the loop, and tie the threads together into a bobble.

LEAF: Use dark green yarn and size E4 (3.5mm) crochet hook.

Crochet 9 ch. Make a turning ch of 2 ch, and crochet like this in 9 ch:

1 dc in first ch, 1 tr in next ch, 2 dtr in next ch, 1 dtr in each of the next 4 ch, 2 dtr in next ch, then like this in last st:

2 tr + 1 dtr + 1 picot (= 2 ch, crochet 1 sl st in the first of these) + 1 dtr + 2 tr. Then cont along the other side of the foundation chain, with sts set like this: 2 dtr in next ch, 1 quad tr in each of the next 4 ch, 2 dtr in next ch, 1 tr in next ch, 1 dc in last ch, 1 sl st at the end of leaf. Crochet another leaf the same but in green yarn.

TO FINISH: Sew the flower to the heart and sew the bobble to the middle of the flower. Paint or color the wooden stake green and let it dry. Stick the stake through the heart. Glue or sew the leaves to the stake. Cut a rectangle out of cardboard, then write your text and glue to the stake.

CARROT

HEART: Cast on with green yarn, and knit the Regular heart (see p. 9).

At the same time, after increasing to 10 sts, knit the color pattern according to the chart.

Fill the finished heart with wadding and sew together any gaps.

OUTER FLOWER: Use cerise yarn and size C2/D3 (3mm) crochet hook.

Crochet a chain 4¾in (12cm) long. Join to make a circle with 1 sl st.

Row 1: Crochet 44 sc into the circle.

Row 2: *1 sl st in first sc, 2 ch, 1 dc in each of the next 2 sc, 2 ch, 1 sl st in next sc*, rep from * to * throughout the row.

MIDDLE FLOWER: Use yellow-orange yarn and size C2/D3 (3mm) crochet hook.

Join 6 ch into a circle with 1 sl st.

Crochet *3 ch + 2 crochet tog tr (see p. 18) + 3 ch + 1sl st*, crochet from * to * a total of five times in the circle. (5 leaves.)

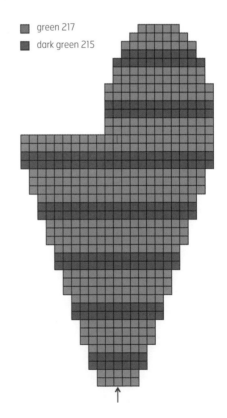

■ green 217
■ dark green 215

Switch to turquoise yarn. Crochet the center of the flower like this: Attach the thread with 1 sl st in circle between two leaves. Crochet 4 ch, *1 dc between the next two leaves*, rep from * to *, close row with 1 sl st in 3rd ch.

TO FINISH: Sew on the outer flower and flower center to the heart. Paint or color the wooden stake green and let it dry. Stick the stake through the heart. Glue or sew the leaves to the stake. Cut a rectangle out of cardboard, then write your text and glue to the stake.

PARSLEY

HEART: Cast on with dark green yarn, and knit the Regular heart (see p. 9).

Fill the finished heart with wadding, and sew together any gaps.

DOTS: Use turquoise yarn held double and embroider knot stitches evenly over the surface of the heart.

LEAF: Use dark green yarn and size E4 (3.5mm) crochet hook.

Crochet 9 ch. Make a turning ch of 2 ch, and crochet like this in the 9 ch:

1 dc in first ch, 1 tr in next ch, 2 dtr in next ch, 1 dtr in each of the next 4 ch, 2 dtr in next ch, then like this in last st: 2 tr + 1 dtr + 1 picot (= 2 ch, crochet 1 sl st in the first one of these) + 1 dtr + 2 tr.

Then cont along the other side of the foundation chain, with sts divided like this: 2 dtr in next ch, 1 quad tr in each of the next 4 ch, 2 dtr in next ch, 1 tr in next ch, 1 dc in last ch, 1 sl st at the end of leaf.

TO FINISH: Paint or color the wooden stake green and let it dry. Stick the stake through the heart. Glue or sew the leaves to the stake. Cut a rectangle out of cardboard, then write your text and glue to the stake.

CUCUMBER

HEART: Cast on with dark green yarn, and knit the Regular heart (see p. 9).

Fill the finished heart with wadding, and sew together any gaps.

DOTS: Use turquoise yarn held double and embroider knot stitches evenly over the surface of the heart.

LEAF: Use dark green yarn and size E4 (3.5mm) crochet hook.

Crochet 9 ch. Make a turning ch of 2 ch, and crochet like this in the 9 ch:

1 dc in first ch, 1 tr in next ch, 2 dtr in next ch, 1 dtr in each of the next 4 ch, 2 dtr in next ch, then like this in last st: 2 tr + 1 dtr + 1 picot (= 2 ch, crochet 1 sl st in the first one of these) + 1 dtr + 2 tr.

Then cont along the other side of the foundation chain, with sts divided like this: 2 dtr in next ch, 1 quad tr in each of the next 4 ch, 2 dtr in next ch, 1 tr in next ch, 1 dc in last ch, 1 sl st at the end of leaf.

TO FINISH: Paint or color the wooden stake green and let it dry. Stick the stake through the heart. Glue or sew the leaves to the stake. Cut a rectangle out of cardboard, then write your text and glue to the stake.

Tip

If the green leaves are a little limp, stiffen them by either spraying on starch or threading a metal wire through the vein of the back of the leaf.

If you are not happy with the handwritten signs, make them on the computer instead. Print (on colored paper if you wish) and cut out. If you want to retain a handwritten feeling, make an uneven frame along the edge of the sign, maybe in the same color as the letters.

A HEAVY HEART IS PROBABLY THE LAST THING YOU WILL FEEL FROM
THESE SPLASHES OF COLOR, BUT WHEN YOU LIFT UP THE HEARTS,
YOU WILL REALIZE THEY ARE SUPRISINGLY HEAVY.

HEAVY HEARTS

NAPKIN HOLDER

HEART MEASUREMENTS: Width 5½ (14cm), height
6¼in (16cm).

MATERIALS:
- Wadding
- Small weights (for example, fishing weights); total
  weight approx. 2oz (60g)
- 1 pack of small cup-shaped flower sequins
- Small transparent rocaille pearls
- 1 yellow butterfly

YARN: Porto (40% cotton, 40% polyacryl, 20%
viscose, 50g = 98yd/90m), some leftovers or 50g
pink/beige/brown 10652.

NEEDLES: US 8 (5mm).

GAUGE: 17 sts x 27 rows = 4 x 4in (10 x 10cm).

♥ ─────────────────────

HEART: Cast on and knit Regular heart (see
p. 9).

Stuff the finished heart with wadding, and
place the weights in the middle of the heart
before you sew up the gaps.

EMBELLISHMENTS: Sew on the sequins
evenly spaced apart. Sew a pearl in the
middle of each sequin.

Attach the butterflies.

The heavy hearts will keep your napkins in place. I've used fishing weights to make them heavy enough, but you can use other types of weights as well.

NAPKIN HOLDER WITH RED BUTTERFLY

HEART MEASUREMENTS: Width 4in (10cm), height 5in (12.5cm).

MATERIALS:
- Wadding
- Small weights (for example fishing weights); total weight approx. 2oz (60g)
- 1 metal clip (for example, curtain clip)
- 1 pack of large flower sequins
- Small green rocaille pearls
- 1 red butterfly

YARN: Thick Magi (70% wool, 30% polyamide, 50g = 136yd/125m), some leftovers or 50g red/orange/pink 5007.

NEEDLES: US 2/3 (3mm).

GAUGE: 24 sts x 34 rows = 4 x 4in (10 x 10cm).

 ♥ ────────────────────

HEART: Cast on, and knit Regular heart (see p. 9).

Stuff the heart with wadding, but leave some space in between the curves of the heart.

TO FINISH: Sew the weight(s) to the metal clip. Thread the heart on the outside of the weights, leaving only the clip to show between the heart curves. Sew up the opening in the heart between the curves.

EMBELLISHMENTS: Sew on the sequins evenly over the heart. Sew a pearl in the middle of each sequin.

Attach the butterfly.

TURQUOISE BUTTERFLY

HEART MEASUREMENTS: Width 3¾in (9.5cm), height 4¼in (10.5cm).

MATERIALS:
- Wadding
- Small weights (for example fishing weights); total weight approx. 2oz (60g)
- 1 metal clip (for example, curtain clip)
- 1 pack of large flower sequins
- Small green rocaille pearls
- 1 turquoise butterfly

YARN: Rio (100% polyamide, 50g = 51yd/47m), some leftovers or 50g tutti-frutti 10384.

NEEDLES: US 6 (4mm).

GAUGE: 25 sts x 41 rows =4 x 4in (10 x 10cm).

 ♥ ────────────────────

HEART: Cast on, and knit Regular heart (see p. 9).

Stuff the heart with wadding, but leave some space in between the curves of the heart.

TO FINISH: Sew the weight(s) to the metal clip. Thread the heart on the outside of the weights, leaving only the clip to show between the heart curves. Sew up the opening in the heart between the curves.

EMBELLISHMENTS: Sew on the sequins evenly over the heart. Sew a pearl in the middle of each sequin.

Attach the butterfly.

 Tip — When you are knitting the heavy hearts with a hanger, make sure the hanger is attached to the weights inside. If you attach the hanger only to the heart, not the weights, the heart will be dragged down and go out of shape.

The yarns used are multicolored and make magical-looking patterns while you knit. In addition, all the hearts are decorated with plenty of sequins, pearls, and sparkling butterflies.

If you hang a heavy heart on every corner of your tablecloth, you won't have to retrieve it from the bottom of the garden on a windy day...

I'M MESSY, BUT IT HELPS TO HAVE EVERY ITEM IN ITS REGULAR SPOT. MY PINS DON'T DISAPPEAR SO QUICKLY IF I HAVE THEM SAFELY STUCK IN MY PINCUSHION.

A STING IN THE HEART

ARM PINCUSHION

HEART MEASUREMENTS BEFORE FELTING: Width 4½in (11cm), height 6½in (16.5cm).

HEART MEASUREMENTS AFTER FELTING: Width 3½in (9cm), height 5¼in (13cm).

MATERIALS:

- Wadding
- Black elastic 15¾in (40cm) long and 1¼in (3cm) wide
- Small piece of black hook-and-loop fastener
- Detergent for felting

YARN: Embla HIFA 3 (100% wool, 100g = 229yd/210m), 50g black 6053 and purple-pink 6076, plus some leftovers or 50g dark cyclamen 6062.

NEEDLES: US 6 (4mm).

GAUGE: 22 sts x 26 rows = 4 x 4in (10 x 10cm) before felting.

HEART: Cast on with purple-pink yarn, and knit Regular heart (see p. 9). At the same time, after increasing to 10 sts, knit the color pattern following the chart below.

Stuff the finished heart with wadding and sew up any gaps.

FELTING: Machine-wash on 60°C with detergent – wash twice if the heart doesn't shrink and felt enough the first time. Shape into a heart while it is still damp.

EMBROIDERY: Using dark cyclamen yarn held double, embroider knot stitches evenly over the front of the heart.

TO FINISH: Sew the hook-and-loop fastener to each end of the elastic and sew on the heart.

♥ ——————————————————————

Pincushions can also disappear! You will avoid that happening with this version – a pincushion that you can strap to your arm so you can take it everywhere.

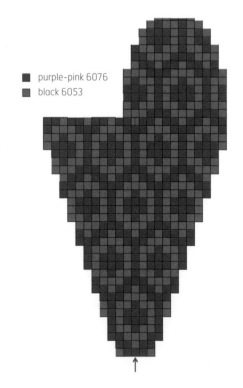

■ purple-pink 6076
■ black 6053

A small, decorative all-in-one workbox! Your tape measure and bobbins will fit inside the box, while the pincushion sits on top. Practical? Yes!

PINCUSHION ON BOX

HEART MEASUREMENTS BEFORE FELTING:
4½in (11cm), height 6½in (16.5cm).

HEART MEASUREMENTS AFTER FELTING: Width 3½in (9cm), height 5¼in (13cm).

MATERIALS:

- Wadding
- Box
- Glue (glue gun)

YARN: Embla HIFA 3 (100% wool, 100g = 229yd/210m), 50g black 6053 and turquoise 6031. Some leftovers or 50g dark blue-purple 6078.

NEEDLES: US 6 (4mm).

GAUGE: 22 sts x 26 rows = 4 x 4in (10 x 10cm) before felting.

 ————————————————————

HEART: Cast on with black yarn, and knit Regular heart (see p. 9). At the same time, after increasing to 10 sts, knit the color pattern following the chart shown right.

Stuff the finished heart with wadding and sew up any gaps.

FELTING: Machine-wash on 60°C with detergent. Wash the heart twice if it doesn't felt enough the first time. Shape into a heart while it is still damp.

EMBROIDERY: Using dark blue-purple yarn held double, embroider knot stitches evenly over the front of the heart.

TO FINISH: Glue the heart to the box.

(see p. 9)

Tip
- Be careful when you felt as the effect of the felting can vary from machine to machine. Felt too little rather than too much; if you wish to felt the heart some more, you can wash it again.
- If you are only felting one or two hearts, put a towel in the machine together with the hearts to make the felting more effective.

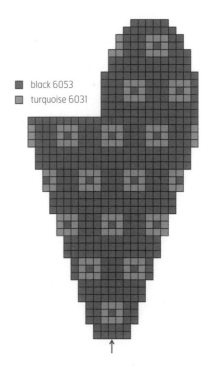

■ black 6053
■ turquoise 6031

HAVE SOMETHING TO SAY? SAY IT WITH WORDS, FLOWERS, OR WITH
FUN MAGNETIC MESSAGES LEFT ON THE REFRIGERATOR.

MAGNETIC HEARTS

FRIDGE MAGNETS

HEART MEASUREMENTS: Width 4¼in (10.5cm), height (6¾in) 17cm.

MATERIALS:
- Wadding
- Magnet
- Glue (glue gun)
- Tags, buttons, and pictures of your choice

YARN: Mitu (50% alpaca, 50% wool, 50g = 109yd/100m), 50g orange 0784 and green 6315.

NEEDLES: US 4 (3.5mm).

GAUGE: 23 sts x 31 rows = 4 x 4in (10 x 10cm).

♥ ────────────────

Make one heart magnet in orange and one in green.

HEART: Cast on and knit a Long heart (see p. 9). Stuff the finished heart with wadding and sew up any gaps.

TO FINISH: Glue the magnet to the back of the heart. Attach tags, buttons, and pictures to the front of the heart.

The pictures and messages will "make" these hearts, which are in themselves just plain and simple. Magnets glued to the back make it possible to stick the hearts to the fridge, the dishwasher, a cookie jar, or a metal lamp.

IS THE WAY TO THE HEART THROUGH THE STOMACH? I DON'T KNOW, BUT EVERYBODY NEEDS FOOD – AND POTHOLDERS ARE HANDY TO HAVE WHEN PREPARING DELICIOUS MEALS. NOW I'M HUNGRY!

THE WAY TO THE HEART

STRIPED POTHOLDER: THE WAY TO A MAN'S HEART

HEART MEASUREMENTS: Width 8in (20.5cm), height 9½in (24cm).

MATERIALS:
- Small piece of fabric (cotton or linen) in light turquoise
- Turquoise sewing thread

YARN (FOR 1 POTHOLDER): All-Year yarn (100% cotton, 50g = 87yd/80m), 50g in each of red 259, pink 248, orange 278, and turquoise 267.

NEEDLES: US 10½/11 (7mm), plus K10½/L11 (7mm) crochet hook.

GAUGE: 12 sts x 18 rows with yarn held double = 4 x 4in (10 x 10cm).

♥ ——————————————————————

HEART: Cast on with red yarn held double, and knit the Regular heart (see p. 9). At the same time, after increasing to 10 sts, knit the color pattern following the chart below. Note! Do not stitch together the gap at the top of the curves of the heart.

CROCHET BORDER: Use a single strand in turquoise.

Row 1: Attach the yarn with sc at the edge (stick down around 2 sts at the side). *Crochet 2 ch, skip approx. ⅜in (1cm) at the edge, 1 sc at the edge*, rep from* to *, but leave out 2 ch at the bottom between the

curves. At the end of the row, replace the last sc with 1 sl st in the first st.

Row 2: Crochet 2 sc in each 2-ch. Close the row with 1 sl st in first st.

EMBELLISHMENTS: Cut a piece of fabric 2¼ x 7¼in (5.5 x 18.5cm); these measurements include ⅜in (1cm) seam allowance along all edges. Fold the seam allowance against the WS and press. Using turquoise yarn held double, embroider the desired text in backstitch (see p. 125 for template), press, and sew the rectangle to front of heart with large basting stitches just inside the edge.

LOOP: Cut a piece of fabric 1½ x 6¼in (4 x 16cm); these measurements include ⅜in (1cm) seam allowance along all edges. Fold the seam allowance against the WS, and fold the loop double lengthwise into a slim loop with a width of ⅜in (1cm). Press. Using the turquoise yarn held double, embroider large basting stitches along the edge. Sew the loop to the potholder.

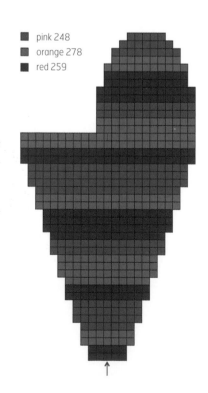

- ■ pink 248
- ■ orange 278
- ■ red 259

The potholders are knitted with the yarn held double and a light gauge. That makes them firm and thick so they will protect you from hot surfaces.

POTHOLDER WITH FLOWER

HEART MEASUREMENTS: Width 8in (20.5cm), height 9½in (24cm).

YARN (FOR 1 POTHOLDER): All-year yarn (100% cotton, 50g = 87yd/80m), 50g in each of pink 248, orange 278, and apple green 280.

NEEDLES: US 10½/11 (7mm), plus K10½ (7mm) crochet hook.

GAUGE: 12 sts x 18 rows with yarn held double = 4 x 4in (10 x 10cm).

♥ —————————————————————————

■ pink 248
■ orange 278

HEART: Cast on in pink yarn held double and knit the Regular heart (see p. 9). At the same time, after increasing to 10 sts, knit the color pattern following the chart shown below left. Note! Do not stitch together the gap at the top of the heart curves.

CROCHET BORDER: Use single strand of green yarn.

Row 1: Attach the yarn with 1 sc to the edge (stick down around 2 sts at the side). *Crochet 2 ch, skip approx. ⅜in (1cm) at the edge, 1 sc at the edge*, rep from * to * but leave out the 2 ch at the bottom between the curves of the heart. Replace the last sc with 1 sl st in the first st at the end of the row.

Row 2: Crochet 2 sc in each 2-ch. Close the row with 1 sl st in the first st.

CROCHET FLOWER: Use two strands of green yarn held together. Join 5 ch to make a circle with 1 sl st.

Row 1: Crochet (4 ch, 1 sc in the circle) five times. (5 leaves.)

Row 2: Fold the leaves from 1st row forward, and crochet in the circle from the back of the flower. Attach the yarn with 1 sl st between two sc (= in the middle of a leaf), *crochet 6 ch, 1 sc in the middle of the next leaf*, repeat from * to * throughout the row. Sew the flower to the center of the potholder.

LOOP: Use two strands of green yarn held double. Crochet 16 ch, turn, and crochet 1 sl st in each ch. Sew the loop to the potholder.

GINGERBREAD POTHOLDER

HEART MEASUREMENTS: Width 8in (20cm), height 8¾in (22.5cm).

YARN (FOR 1 POTHOLDER): Sumatra (100% cotton, 50g = 93yd/85m), 100g brown 3008 and some leftovers or 50g white 3003.

NEEDLES: US 10 (6mm) plus E4 (3.5mm) and I9 (5.5mm) crochet hooks.

GAUGE: 12 sts x 19 rows with the yarn held double = 4 x 4in (10 x 10cm).

♥ ————————————————

HEART: Cast on with brown yarn held double and knit the Regular heart (see p. 9). Note! Do not stitch together the gap at the top of the heart curves.

CROCHET BORDER: Use I9 (5.5mm) crochet hook and a single strand of brown yarn.

Row 1: Attach the yarn with 1 sc at the edge (stick down around 2 sts at the side). *Crochet 2 ch, skip approx. ⅜in (1cm) at the edge, 1 sc at the edge*, rep from * to * but leave out the 2 ch at the bottom between the curves of the heart. Replace the last sc with 1 sl st in the first st at the end of the row.

Row 2: Crochet 2 sc in each 2-ch. Close the row with 1 sl st in first st.

"FROSTING" EMBELLISHMENT: Use E4

(3.5mm) crochet hook and a single strand of white yarn. Using the illustration as a guide, crochet chain, and sew this to the front of the potholder as a border right inside the heart outline and as a gingerbread motif in the middle of the heart. Embroider eyes and buttons with knot stitch, and the mouth with knit stitch.

LOOP: Use I9 (5.5mm) crochet hook and brown yarn held double.

Crochet 18 ch, turn, and crochet 1 sl st in each ch. Sew the loop to the potholder.

NORWEGIAN ROSE POTHOLDER

HEART MEASUREMENTS: Width 8in (20cm), height 9in (22.5cm).

YARN (FOR 1 POTHOLDER): Sumatra (100% cotton, 50g = 93yd/85m), 100g black 3014; Petunia (100% cotton, 50g = 120yd/110m), some leftovers or 50g red 256, green 215, salmon 245, blue 275, turquoise 275, and purple 260.

NEEDLES: US 10 (6mm) plus size 7 (4.5mm) crochet hook.

GAUGE: 12 sts x 19 rows with Sumatra yarn held double = 4 x 4in (10 x 10cm).

♥ ──────────────────────────────

HEART: Cast on with black yarn held double and knit the Regular heart (see p. 9). Note! Do not stitch together the gap at the top of the heart curves.

CROCHET BORDER: Use red yarn held double.

Row 1: Attach the yarn with 1 sc at the edge (stick down around 2 sts at the side). *Crochet 2 ch, skip approx. ⅜in (1cm) at the edge, 1 sc at the edge*, rep from * to * but leave out the 2 ch at the bottom between the curves of the heart. Replace the last sc with 1 sl st in the first st at the end of the row.

Row 2: Switch to green yarn held double. Crochet 2 sc in each 2-ch. Close the row with 1 sl st in the first st.

EMBROIDERY: Using the illustration as a guide, embroider the Norwegian rose motif on the front of the heart; embroider freehand, or baste a few stitches for guidance before you begin.

LOOP: Use green yarn held double.

Crochet 18 ch, turn, and crochet 1 sl st in each ch. Sew the loop to the potholder.

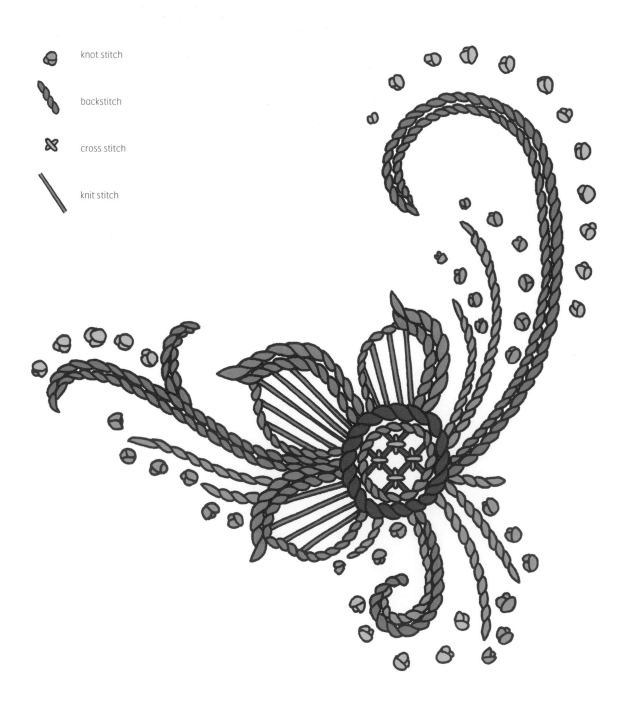

knot stitch

backstitch

cross stitch

knit stitch

POTHOLDER WITH BOBBLES

HEART MEASUREMENTS: Width 8in (20cm), height 9in (22.5cm).

YARN (FOR 1 POTHOLDER): Sumatra (100% cotton, 50g = 93yd/85m), 100g red 3044 and some leftovers or 50g white 3003.

NEEDLES: US 10 (6mm) plus G6 (4mm) and I9 (5.5mm) crochet hooks.

GAUGE: 12 sts x 19 rows with yarn held double = 4 x 4in (10 x 10cm).

CROCHET TOG DTR: Crochet each dtr, but leave out the last one. When you crochet the last dtr, pull the thread through all the loops on the hook.

♥ ————————————————————

HEART: Cast on with red yarn held double and knit Regular heart (see p. 9). Note! Do not stitch together the gap at the top of the heart curves.

CROCHET BORDER: Use a single strand of white yarn and I9 (5.5mm) crochet hook.

Row 1: Attach the yarn with 1 sc at the edge (stick down around 2 sts at the side). *Crochet 2 ch, skip approx. ⅜in (1cm) at the edge, 1 sc at the edge*, rep from * to * but leave out the 2 ch at the bottom between the curves of the heart. Replace the last sc with 1 sl st in the first st at the end of the row.

Row 2: Crochet 2 sc in each 2-ch. Close the row with 1 sl st in first st.

BOBBLES: Use G6 (4mm) crochet hook and a single strand of white yarn.

Make a loose loop. Crochet 3 ch, then crochet tog 4 dtr (see instructions above) in the loop. Cut the yarn. Tighten the loose loop and tie the end of the threads together, into a bobble. Crochet 8 bobbles like this and sew them evenly spaced to the front of the heart.

LOOP: Use I9 (5.5mm) crochet hook and white yarn held double.

Crochet 18 ch, turn, and crochet 1 sl st in each ch. Sew the loop to the potholder.

POTHOLDER WITH EIGHT-PETAL ROSE

HEART MEASUREMENTS: Width 8in (20cm), height 9in (22.5cm).

YARN (FOR 1 POTHOLDER): Sumatra (100% cotton, 50g = 93yd/85m), 100g red 3044 and some leftovers or 50g white 3003.

NEEDLES: US 10 (6mm) plus I9 (5.5mm) crochet hook.

GAUGE: 12 sts x 19 rows with yarn held double = 4 x 4in (10 x 10cm).

♥ ────────────────────────────

HEART: Cast on with red yarn held double and knit Regular heart (see p. 9). Note! Do not stitch together the gaps at the top of the heart curves.

CROCHET BORDER: Use a single strand of white yarn.

Row 1: Attach the yarn with 1 sc at the edge (stick down around 2 sts at the side). *Crochet 2 ch, skip approx. ⅜in (1cm) at the edge, 1 sc at the edge*, rep from * to *, but leave out the 2 ch at the bottom between the curves of the heart. Replace the last sc with 1 sl st in the first st at the end of the row.

Row 2: Crochet 2 sc in each 2-ch. Close the row with 1 sl st in the first st.

EMBROIDERY: Using the illustration as a guide and holding the white yarn double, embroider the long stitches to make the rose motif; use a blunt tapestry needle or a crochet hook to pull the yarn through sts.

LOOP: Use white yarn held double. Crochet 18 ch, turn, and crochet 1 sl st in each ch. Sew the loop to the potholder.

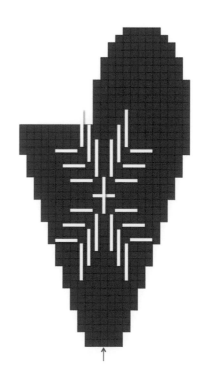

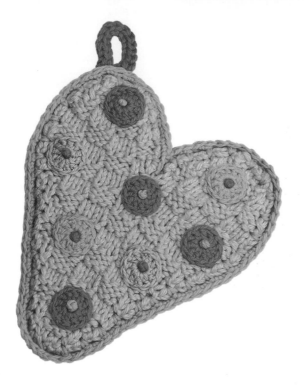

POTHOLDER WITH DOTS

HEART MEASUREMENTS: Width 8in (20.5cm), height 9½in (24cm).

YARN (FOR 1 POTHOLDER): All-Year yarn (100% cotton, 50g = 87yd/80m), 100g yellow 206 and some leftovers or 50g in each of pink 248, orange 278, apple green 280, and turquoise 267.

NEEDLES: US 10½/11 (7mm) plus G6 (4mm) and K10½/11 (7mm) crochet hooks.

GAUGE: 12 sts x 18 rows with yarn held double = 4 x 4in (10 x 10cm).

♥ ────────────────────

HEART: Cast on with yellow yarn held double and knit Regular heart (see p. 9). At the same time, after increasing to 10 sts, knit the color pattern following the chart left. Note! Do not stitch together the gaps at the top of the heart curves.

CROCHET BORDER: Use K10½/11 (7mm) crochet hook and a single strand of turquoise yarn.

Row 1: Attach the thread with 1 sc at the edge (stick down around 2 sts at the side). *Crochet 2 ch, skip approx. ⅜in (1cm) at the edge, 1 sc at the edge*, rep from * to * but leave out the 2 ch at the bottom between the curves of the heart. Replace the last sc with 1 sl st in the first st at the end of the row.

Row 2: Crochet 2 sc in each 2-ch. Close the row with 1 sl st in the first st.

CROCHET DOTS: Use G6 (4mm) crochet hook and a single strand of yarn.

Crochet two circles in each of pink, orange, apple green, and turquoise like this:

Join 4 ch in a circle with 1 sl st.

Crochet 2 ch (= 1st dc), then make 11 dc in the circle. Finish with 1 sl st at the top of 1st dc. Sew the circles tight and then space them out evenly over the front of the heart, and sew knot stitches in contrasting colors in the middle of each dot.

LOOP: Use K10½/11 (7mm) crochet hook and orange yarn held double. Crochet 18 ch, turn, and crochet 1 sl st in each ch. Sew the loop to the potholder.

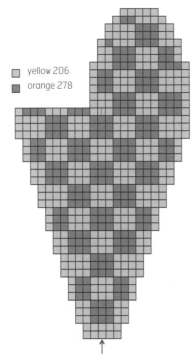

□ yellow 206
■ orange 278

Heart's choice

LAILA (designer)
How could I not smile with these joyful potholders in the kitchen?

POTHOLDER WITH EMBROIDERED APPLE

HEART MEASUREMENTS: Width 8in (20.5cm), height 9½in (24cm).

YARN (FOR 1 POTHOLDER): All-Year yarn (100% cotton, 50g = 87yd/80m), 100g apple green 280; Sumatra (100% cotton, 50g = 93yd/85m), some leftovers or 50g in each of red 3044, brown 3008, and green 3295.

NEEDLES: US 10½/11 (7mm) plus G6 (4mm) and K10½/11 (7mm) crochet hooks.

GAUGE: 12 sts x 18 rows with All-Year yarn held double = 4 x 4in (10 x 10cm).

♥ ─────────────────────────────

HEART: Cast on with green yarn held double and knit Regular heart (see p. 9). Note! Do not stitch together the gaps at the top of the heart curves.

CROCHET BORDER: Use K10½/11 (7mm) crochet hook and a single strand of apple green yarn.

Row 1: Attach the yarn with 1 sc at the edge (stick down around 2 sts at the side). *Crochet 2 ch, skip approx. ⅜in (1cm) at the edge, 1 sc at the edge*, rep from * to *, but leave out the 2 ch at the bottom between the curves of the heart. Replace the last sc with 1 sl st in the first st at the end of the row.

Row 2: Crochet 2 sc in each 2-ch. Close the row with 1 sl st in the first st.

EMBROIDERY: Using the chart as a guide, embroider the apple motif on the front of the potholder. Embroider kitchener stitch using the red yarn held double and a blunt tapestry needle.

EMBROIDERED LEAF: Use G6 (4mm) crochet hook and a single strand of green yarn.

Cast on 9 ch. Turn with 2 ch and cont like this:

1 dc in first ch, 1 tr in next ch, 2 dtr in next ch, 1 dtr in each of the next 4 ch, 2 dtr in next ch, then like this in the last st: 2 tr + 1 dtr + 1 picot (= 2 ch, crochet 1 sl st in the first of these) + 1 dtr + 2 tr. Then cont along the other side of the foundation chain, with sts divided like this: 2 dtr in next ch, 1 quad tr in each of the next 4 ch, 2 dtr in next ch, 1 tr in next ch, 1 dc in next ch in last ch, 2 ch, 1 sl st at the end of the leaf.

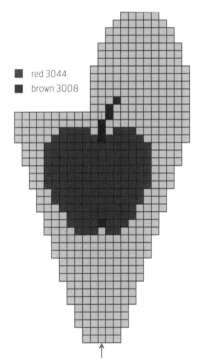

■ red 3044
■ brown 3008

Sew the leaf to the potholder by the apple stalk.

LOOP: Use K10½/11 (7mm) crochet hook and apple green yarn held double. Crochet 18 ch, turn, and crochet 1 sl st in each ch. Sew the loop to the potholder.

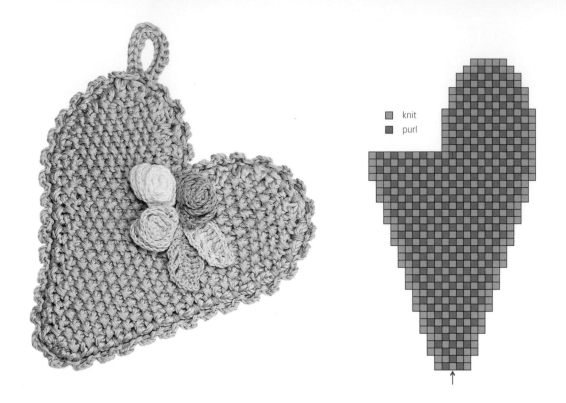

knit
purl

POTHOLDER WITH CROCHET FLOWERS

HEART MEASUREMENTS: Width 8in (20cm), height 8½in (21.5cm).

YARN (FOR 1 POTHOLDER): Sumatra (100% cotton, 50g = 93yd/85m), 100g light old rose 3030; Pandora (100% cotton, 50g = 197yd/180m), some leftovers or 50g in each of white 296, light pink 231, pink 232, light green 215, and mint 282.

NEEDLES: US 10 (6mm) plus C2/D3 (3mm) and I9 (5.5mm) crochet hooks.

GAUGE: 12 sts x 20 rows with yarn held double using Sumatra and seed stitch patt = 4 x 4in (10 x 10cm).

SMALL PETAL: 3 ch, 1 dc in each of the 2 next ch, 2 ch, 1 sl st in next st.

MEDIUM PETAL: 4 ch, 1 dtr in each of the 4 next ch, 3 ch, 1 sl st in next st.

LARGE PETAL: 4 ch, 1 dtr in each of the 6 next ch, 3 ch, 1 sl st in next st.

♥ ————————————————————

HEART: Cast on with light old rose yarn held double and knit Regular heart (see p. 9). At the same time, after increasing to 10 sts, knit the seed stitch pattern following the chart above. Note! Do not stitch together the gaps at the top of the heart curves.

CROCHET BORDER: Use pink yarn held double and I9 (5.5mm) crochet hook.

Row 1: Attach the thread with 1 sc at the edge (stick down around 2 sts at the side).

Crochet 2 ch, skip approx. ⅜in (1cm) at the edge, 1 sc at the edge, rep from * to * but leave out the 2 ch at the bottom between the curves of the heart. Replace the last sc with 1 sl st in the first st at the end of the row.

Row 2: Switch to mint yarn held double. Crochet 1 sl st + 3 ch + 1 sl st in each 2 ch.

LOOP: Use light old rose yarn held double and I9 (5.5mm) crochet hook. Crochet 18 ch, turn, and crochet 1 sl st in each ch. Sew the loop to the potholder.

ROSES: Crochet 1 of each in pink, light pink, and white. Use a single strand of yarn and C2/D3 (3mm) crochet hook. Make a chain of 52 sts. Turn, and crochet three small petals (see instructions left), three medium petals, and four large petals. Roll the row with petals into a spiral, with the smallest petals farthest in. Sew tog at the bottom edge as you roll.

LEAVES: Crochet 1 of each in mint and light green. Use a single strand of yarn and C2/D3 (3mm) crochet hook. Cast on 14 ch: 1sc in each of the 2 first ch, 1 sl st in each of the next two, 2 ch, 1 dc in the next ch, 2 ch, 1 dtr in next ch, 2 ch, skip 1 ch, 1 dtr in next ch, 2 ch, skip 1 ch, 1 dc in next ch, 1 ch, skip 1 ch, 1 tr in next ch, 1 sc in next ch, 1 sl st in last ch, turn to other side of the foundation chain with 2 ch, skip 1st ch, and crochet 1 st in each st divided like this: 1 sc, 1 dc, 5 dtr, 1 dc. Crochet 2 ch and 1 sl st in next st.

TO FINISH: Sew flowers and leaves to the front of the potholder.

POTHOLDER WITH EMBROIDERED ROSE

HEART MEASUREMENTS: Width 8in (20cm), height 9in (22.5cm).

YARN (FOR 1 POTHOLDER): Sumatra (100% cotton, 50g = 93yd/85m), 100g white 3003; Pandora (100% cotton, 50g = 197yd/180m), some leftovers or 50g in each of light green 215, green 280, light pink 232, and pink 251.

NEEDLES: US 10 (6mm) plus I9 (5.5mm) crochet hook.

GAUGE: 12 sts x 19 rows with Sumatra yarn held double = 4 x 4in (10 x 10cm).

♥ ——————————————————————

HEART: Cast on with white yarn held double and knit Regular heart (see p. 9). Note! Do not stitch together the gaps at the top of the heart curves.

CROCHET BORDER: Use a single strand of white yarn.

Row 1: Attach the yarn with 1 sc at the edge (stick down around 2 sts at the side). *Crochet 2 ch, skip approx. ⅜in (1cm) at the edge, 1 sc at the edge*, rep from * to *, but leave out the 2 ch at the bottom between the curves of the heart. Replace the last sc with 1 sl st in the first st at the end of the row.

Row 2: Crochet 1 sl st + 3 ch + 1 sl st in each 2 ch.

EMBROIDERY: Using the chart as a guide, embroider the rose motif to the front of the potholder. Embroider cross stitches using the yarn held double and a blunt tapestry needle.

LOOP: Use the white yarn held double. Crochet 18 ch, turn, and crochet 1 sl st in each ch. Sew the loop to the potholder.

light pink 232
pink 251
light green 215
green 280

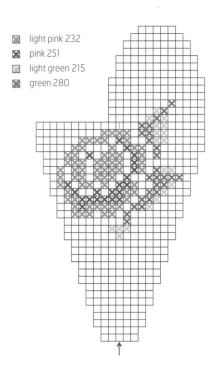

Young hearts

HAIR DECORATIONS

HEART HAIRCLIP

HEART MEASUREMENTS: Width 2½in (6.5cm),
height 3½in (9cm).

MATERIALS:
- Wadding
- Hairclip
- Foam stickers
- Glue (glue gun)

YARN: Plum (70% mohair, 30% polyamide, 25g
= 273yd/250m), some leftovers or 25g pink 107;
Metallic (45% polyamide, 55% metallic fiber, 1 bobbin
= 1093yd/1000m), 1 bobbin pink 313.

NEEDLES: US 0 (2mm).

GAUGE: 38 sts x 60 rows with 1 strand each of Plum
and Metallic = 4 x 4in (10 x 10cm).

♥ ————————————————————

HEART: Cast on using one strand of each
yarn, and knit Long heart (see p. 9).

Fill the finished heart with wadding, and
sew up any gaps.

TO FINISH: Glue or sew the heart to the
hairclip and glue stickers on the heart. Use
adhesive on the stickers – they need extra
grip to stick to this kind of base, even if they
are self-adhesive.

HEART HEADBAND

HEART MEASUREMENTS: Width 2½in (6.5cm),
height 3½in (9cm).

MATERIALS:
- Wadding
- Plastic headband
- Foam stickers
- 39in (1m) of pink sateen ribbon
- Glue (glue gun)

YARN: Plum (70% mohair, 30% polyamide, 25g =
273yd/250m), some leftovers or 25g purple 053;
Metallic (45% polyamide, 55% metallic fiber, 1 bobbin
= 1093yd/1000m), 1 bobbin purple 312.

NEEDLE SUGGESTION: US 0 (2mm).

GAUGE: 38 sts x 60 rows with 1 strand each of Plum
and Metallic = 4 x 4in (10 x 10cm).

♥ ————————————————————

HEART: Cast on using one strand of each
yarn, and knit Long heart (see p. 9).

Fill the finished heart with wadding, and
sew up any gaps.

TO FINISH: Wind the sateen ribbon around
the headband and attach securely at both
sides. Glue the heart on to the headband,
and glue stickers to the heart and diadem.
Use adhesive on the stickers – they need
extra grip to stick to this kind of base, even
if they are self-adhesive.

The hearts are knitted in mohair, thin as a spider's web, held together with a yarn that has some sparkle to it. The hearts are sewn or glued to the headband or hairclip, together with other decorations.

THERE IS SOMETHING MAGICAL ABOUT OWLS. NOT ONLY DO THEY HAVE A REPUTATION FOR BEING WISE AND INTELLIGENT, THEY ALSO HAVE A FASCINATING LOOK, WHICH IS INSPIRING!

OWLS

PURPLE OWL

HEART MEASUREMENTS: Width 3½in (9cm), height 6in (15cm).

MATERIALS:
- Wadding
- 2 plastic eyes, diameter ¾in (20mm)
- Copper-colored metal thread 0.5 mm
- Transparent thread
- Glue

YARN: Ask HIFA 2 (100% wool, 100g = 344yd/315m), some leftovers or 50g in each of purple 6078, turquoise 6031, blue-purple 6063, and ocher 6095.

NEEDLES: US ½ (2.5mm).

GAUGE: 27 sts x 35 rows = 4 x 4in (10 x 10cm).

♥ ──────────────────────

BODY: Cast on with ocher yarn and knit Long heart (see p. 9).

After increasing to 10 sts, knit color pattern as shown in chart right.

Fill the finished heart with wadding; don't put too much at the bottom by the tip of the heart (= owl's head). Sew together the seam between the curves of the heart.

Fold the bottom 1¼in (3cm) of the heart upward, and attach with stitches to make the owl's head. Sew or glue on the eyes.

TUMMY: Using turquoise yarn, cast on 5 sts. Work in st st back and forth, at the same time increasing at each side on every other row: 2 sts once, 1 st two times. (13 sts.) Knit until the work measures 1¼in (3cm). Then bind off 1 st of each side in alt rows: 1 st two times, 2 sts once (5 sts). Bind off. Sew the tummy to the front of the owl.

WINGS: Using blue-purple yarn, cast on 3 sts. Work in st st back and forth. On the 3rd row, inc by 1 st at each side. Rep this inc on every 4th row until there are 9 sts on the row. Knit until work measures 2in (5cm). Then bind off 1 st at each side on every row until there are 3 sts on the row. Bind off. Knit another wing. Sew the wings to the owl, one on each side by the shoulders.

FEET: Use the metal thread held double and wind to make two feet with three toes (use photograph as a guide). Insert one in each heart curve at the bottom of the owl. Attach with a few stitches or glue.

HANGER: Attach transparent thread on top as a hanger.

■ ocher 6095
■ purple 6078
■ turquoise 6031

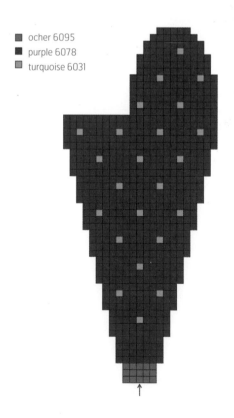

A purple owl? A brown owl? Or pick the color you want. This yarn is available in nearly 80 different color shades, so the possibilities are nearly endless.

BROWN OWL

HEART MEASUREMENTS: Width 3½in (9cm), height 6in (15cm).

MATERIALS:
- Wadding
- 2 plastic eyes, diameter ¾in (20mm)
- Copper-colored metal thread 0.5 mm
- Transparent thread
- Glue

YARN: Ask HIFA 2 (100% wool, 100g = 344yd/315m), some leftovers or 50g in each of brown 6099, blue-green 6029, moss green 6090, and brown-orange 6095.

NEEDLES: US ½ (2.5mm).

GAUGE: 27 sts x 35 rows = 4 x 4in (10 x 10cm).

♥ ──────────────────────────

BODY: Cast on with brown-orange yarn and knit Long heart (see p. 9). After increasing to 10 sts, knit the color pattern following the chart right.

Fill the finished heart with wadding; don't put too much at the bottom by the tip of the heart (= owl's head). Sew together the seam between the curves of the heart. Fold the bottom 1¼in (3cm) of the heart upward, and attach with stitches to make the owl's head. Sew or glue on the eyes.

TUMMY: Using blue-green yarn, cast on 5 sts. Work in st st back and forth, at the same time increasing at each side on every other row: 2 sts once, 1 st two times. (13 sts.) Knit until the work measures 1¼in (3cm). Then bind off 1 st of each side in alt rows: 1 st two times, 2 sts once (5 sts). Bind off. Sew the tummy to the front of the owl.

WINGS: Using moss green yarn, cast on 3 sts. Work in st st back and forth. On the 3rd row, inc by 1 st at each side. Rep this inc on every 4th row until there are 9 sts on the row. Knit

until the work measures 2in (5cm). Then bind off 1 st at each side on every row until there are 3 sts on the row. Bind off. Knit another wing. Sew the wings to the owl, one on each side by the shoulders.

FEET: Use the metal thread held double and wind to make two feet with three toes (use photograph as a guide). Insert one in each heart curve at the bottom of the owl. Attach with a few stitches or glue.

HANGER: Attach transparent thread on top as a hanger.

■ brown-orange 6096
■ brown 6099
■ blue-green 6029

TUTTI FRUTTI

SEED STITCH CUSHION

HEART MEASUREMENTS: Width 19in (48cm),
height 21¼in (54cm).

MATERIALS:
• Wadding

YARN: Ara (100% wool, 50g = 55yd/50m), 750g
purple 5036; Falk (100% wool, 50g = 116yd/106m),
some leftovers or 50g in each of orange 3309,
apple green 8817, green 8426, and turquoise 6215.

NEEDLES: US 36 (20mm), plus size 7 (4.5mm)
crochet hook.

GAUGE: 5 sts x 8 rows using six strands of yarn held
together and seed stitch = 4 x 4in (10 x 10cm).

CROCHET TOG 3-DTR: Crochet each 3-dtr, but
leave out the last one. When you crochet the last
3-dtr, pull the thread through all the loops on the
hook.

♥ ————————————————————

HEART: Cast on with six strands of yarn held
together, and knit Long heart (see p. 9).

After increasing to 10 sts, knit the seed stitch
pattern following the chart right.

Fill the finished heart with wadding, and
sew up any gaps.

FLOWER: Use orange yarn held double.
Crochet a chain 79in (2m) long. Switch to
apple green yarn and crochet further 79in
(2m), then switch to green yarn and crochet
further 79in (2m). Finish, and leave 12–
15¾in (30–40cm) at the end of the yarn. Sew
a basting stitch for every 4–4¾in (10–12cm)
along the whole chain. Pull the yarn along
the way, so the chain forms loops. When the
chain changes color, make sure the basting
stitch is right by the color change. When the
whole chain is sewn into loops, pull the yarn
and attach. Arrange the loops into a flower,
with orange furthest in and green furthest

out. Sew tightly together underneath.

FLOWER CENTER: Use turquoise yarn held
double. Make a loose loop. Crochet 3 ch,
then crochet tog 4 3-dtr (see directions left)
in the loop. Cut the yarn. Tighten the loose
loop, and tie the threads into a bobble.

TO FINISH: Sew the flower center to the
flower, and attach the flower to the middle
of the pillow all through the heart.

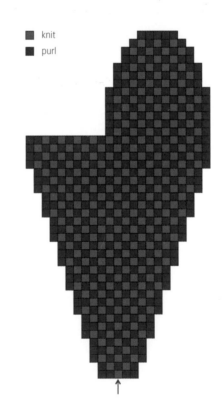

■ knit
■ purl

The purple cushion is made in seed stitch, the green and turquoise version is turned inside out, while the candy-colored cushion is left right side out – simple variations with lovely final results. The flower on the purple pillow doesn't require much crochet skill; it consists of a long string of crochet chain, which is sewn into loops and stitched in place.

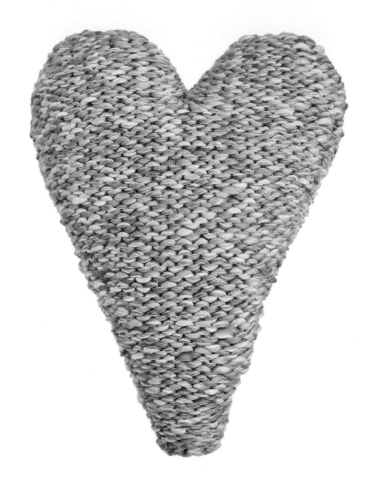

INSIDE-OUT CUSHION

HEART MEASUREMENTS: Width 19in (48cm), height 26in (66cm).

MATERIALS:
• Wadding

YARN: Ara (100% wool, 50g = 55yd/50m), 800g turquoise-green 35315.

NEEDLES: US 36 (20mm).

GAUGE: 5 sts x 8 rows using six strands of yarn held together = 4 x 4in (10 x 10cm).

♥ ────────────────────────────

Cast on with six strands of yarn held together, and knit Long heart (see p. 9).

Turn the finished heart inside out, fill with wadding, and sew up any gaps.

CANDY-COLORED CUSHION

HEART MEASUREMENTS: Width 21in (53.5cm), height 24in (61.5cm).

MATERIALS:
• Wadding

YARN: HIFA Troll yarn (100% wool, 50g = 55yd/50m), 150g in each of orange 711, dark orange 712, red 719, deep pink 736, purple-pink 721, tart green 730, and blue-turquoise 727.

NEEDLES: US 36 (20mm).

GAUGE: 4.5 sts x 7 rows with seven strands of yarn held together = 4 x 4in (10 x 10cm).

♥ —————————————————————————

Cast on with one strand of yarn in each color (= seven strands altogether), and knit Regular heart (see p.9).

Fill the finished heart with wadding, and sew together the gaps between the curves of the heart.

Heart's choice

BENTE
(that's me!)
I like fresh colors and simplicity.
This large, lovely heart offers both –
just the way I like it. Therefore this
cushion is my favorite heart.

FLYING HEARTS

CEILING MOBILE WITH HEARTS

HEART MEASUREMENTS: Width 3¼in (8cm), height 3¾in (9.5cm).

MATERIALS:
- Wadding
- 2 packs of fabric buttons in Fairytale Pink
- 1 ceiling mobile

YARN: Pandora (100% cotton, 50g = 197yd/180m), 50g in each of white 296, light pink 231, pink 232, and light purple 710, and some leftovers or 50g in each of mint 282, apple green 280, turquoise 267, blue 269, and purple 279.

NEEDLES: US½ (2.5mm) plus B1/C2 (2.5mm) crochet hook.

GAUGE: 30 sts x 46 rows = 4 x 4in (10 x 10cm).

♥ ────────────────────────

HEARTS: Make 11 Regular hearts (see p. 9) in these colors: 2 white, 3 light pink, 2 pink, 1 light purple, 1 striped pink/white, 1 striped light pink/pink, and 1 striped light purple/white. For the striped hearts: cast on with the color listed on top in the charts below, and, after increasing to 10 sts, knit color pattern following charts below.

EMBROIDERY: Embroider knot stitches evenly spaced over the white hearts. Using yarn held double, and embroider light pink knots on one of the white hearts and knots in both shades of pink on the other.

BUTTON EMBELLISHMENTS: Sew 1 button to each side of 1 pink heart, 1 white heart, 1 purple heart, 1 striped pink/white heart, 1 striped light pink/pink heart, and 1 striped light purple/white heart.

CROCHET FLOWERS: Crochet 12 flowers using mint, apple green, turquoise, blue, and purple:

Make a loose loop. Crochet (7 ch + sl st) five times in the loop. Tighten the loop, and tie together the ends.

Sew one flower to each side of the hearts without buttons. Each heart should have different color flowers on each side. When attaching the flowers, sew the yarn end from one flower through the heart to the other flower, and embroider a knot in the middle of the flower.

YARN ON THE CEILING MOBILE: Wind yarn around the arms of the mobile, using mint, apple green, turquoise, blue, and purple. Begin at the farthest end of each arm, and attach the yarn by winding the yarn on top of each other. Change colors as you wish. Before you change color, wind the existing color around the new color, and wind the same way with a new color over an old color after a color change. By using small

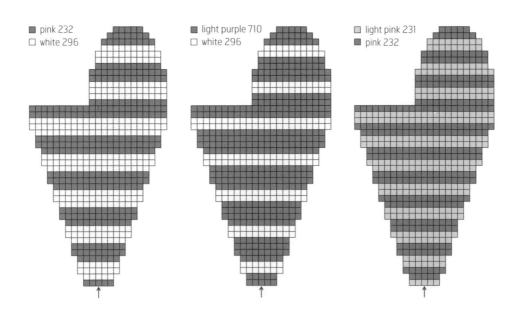

The hearts are made in pastel shades of pink, white, and lilac, while the embellishments and hanging chains are made in green, blue, and purple.

stripes in repeating colors, the color not used may follow underneath the one in use. Cut the yarn and weave the loose ends in through the wound thread at the end of each arm.

CHAINS: Use mint. Crochet a chain 14½in (37cm) long, turn, and make 1 sl st in each ch. Crochet similar chains in each of the colors apple green, turquoise, and blue. Crochet a 17¼in (44cm)-long chain in purple – this will go in the middle.

Place the hearts on the chains; use the picture as a guide or make your own version. Make adjustments if needed. When you are happy with the placement, use a crochet hook to pull the yarn chains through each heart: Begin with the heart that you want at the top, and work your way down. Insert the crochet hook from the bottom upward, and pull the yarn back through the heart. Tie multiple large knots at the bottom of the strings, and hang a string of hearts on each arm of the mobile. Use adhesive to attach if necessary.

HANGER: Use mint. Crochet a chain like the other chains but in the length you require. Attach to the mobile's hanger.

Heart's choice

DANIEL
(my son – who decided on this one long before he saw all of the hearts):

This is the best one, mom! I like the colors; I think they are cool and cute and fun. There's one color I particularly like, and that's the purple. I like the way the hearts are hanging and can turn around.

 Tip Remember to attach all the little parts as tightly as possible so they cannot be ripped off and put in someone's mouth! This is particularly important if the mobile is within a child's reach.

WELCOME TO THE WORLD! THESE HEARTS MAKE GREAT GIFTS FOR A NEWBORN BABY. THEY WILL ALSO LOOK SWEET IN THE NURSERY.

A BRAND NEW HEART

HEART MEASUREMENTS: Width 3¼in (18.5cm), height 9¾in (25cm).

MATERIALS:
- Wadding
- White sateen string
- Ribbon to use for hanging loop

YARN: Sumatra (100% cotton, 50g = 93yd/85m), 100g light blue 3021 and light purple 3022. Some leftovers or 50g white 3003.

NEEDLES: US 10 (6mm) plus G6 (4mm) and I9 (5.5mm) crochet hooks.

GAUGE: 13 sts x 21 rows using yarn held double and seed stitch = 4 x 4in (10 x 10cm).

♥ ————————————————————

Knit one heart in light purple and one in light blue.

HEART: Cast on with yarn held double and knit Long heart (see p. 9). At the same time, after increasing to 10 sts, knit the seed stitch pattern following the charts below. Fill the finished heart with wadding, and sew up any the gaps.

CROCHET BORDER: Use a single strand of white yarn and I9 (5.5mm) crochet hook.

Row 1: Attach the yarn with 1 sc at the edge (stick down around 2 sts at the side). *Crochet 2 ch, skip approx. ⅜in (1cm) at the edge, 1 sc at the edge*, rep from * to *, but leave out the 2 ch at the bottom between the curves of the heart. Replace the last sc with 1 sl st in the first st at the end of the row.

Row 2: Crochet 1 sl st + 3 ch + 1 sl st in each 2 ch.

LETTERS: Use the sateen string and G6 (4mm) crochet hook. Crochet chain to the desired suitable length, arrange them into initials, and sew them the hearts (see Tip).

HANGING LOOP: Sew on a piece of ribbon to use as a hanging loop.

Tip
- If you find it difficult to make the letters look nice, find a font you like on the computer and print the letter you want.
- Embroider the date on the back of the heart.

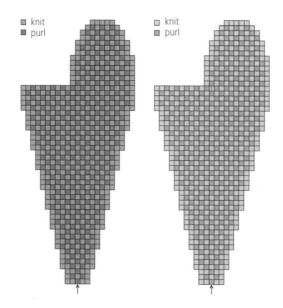

■ knit
■ purl

■ knit
■ purl

D is for Daniel – a little boy with a big place in mom's heart! You can make the letters yourself, like here, or buy them ready-made.

SOMETIMES IT'S OKAY TO TURN THINGS UPSIDE DOWN, WHICH IS
WHAT I'VE DONE HERE. THE HEARTS HAVE BEEN TRANSFORMED INTO A
PROUD MOTHER HEN WITH THREE FLUFFY LITTLE CHICKS.

MOTHER HEN

MOTHER HEN

HEART MEASUREMENTS: Width 5½in (14cm),
height 10½in (26.5cm).

MATERIALS:
- Wadding
- Orange, pink, and apricot rubber
- White fake fur or feathers for wings
- Metal wire to support feet (optional)
- 2 plastic eyes, ¾in (20mm) diameter
- Glue (glue gun)
- Double-sided tape

YARN: Rio (100% polyamide, 50g = 51yd/47m),
50g white 999; Pandora (100% cotton, 50g =
197yd/180m), 50g white 296.

NEEDLES: US 9 (5.5mm).

GAUGE: 17 sts x 20 rows using two strands of Rio
and one of Pandora held together = 4 x 4in (10 x 10
cm).

♥ ────────────────────────

HEART: Cast on with two strands of Rio and
one strand of Pandora held together. Knit
the Long heart (see p. 9). Turn the finished
heart inside out, fill with wadding, and sew
up any gaps.

FEET: Roughly cut out four feet (see p. 125
for template) in apricot rubber. Stick 2 and
2 together using double-sided tape. Trim the
feet with scissors to make them even, then
glue them to the hen using a glue gun. For
extra support, cut short lengths of metal
wire and glue them under each foot.

HEAD: Cut out the comb (see p. 125 for
template) in pink rubber, and the beak in
orange. Sew the comb to the middle of the
head. Fold the beak in half along the dotted
line and attach it to the hen with a few
stitches on each side of the beak. Make a
couple of stitches through the whole beak
in the middle, at the base of the beak, so
the top and bottom parts of the beak stay
together.

Attach the eyes above the beak.

WINGS AND TAIL: Attach a few pieces
of fake fur or feathers on each side for
the wings, and another piece for the tail
feathers.

The mother hen is knitted with smooth yarn to give a feeling of sleek feathers. The chicks are knitted with fluffier yarn.

CHICKS

HEART MEASUREMENTS: Width 3½in (9cm), height 5in (12.5cm).

MATERIALS:
- Wadding
- Orange and apricot rubber
- White, light blue, and pastel purple fake fur or feathers
- Metal wire to support feet (optional)
- 6 plastic eyes, ⅜in (10mm) diameter
- Glue (glue gun)

YARN: Beo (100% polyamide, 50g = 109yd/100m), 50g in each of white 5000, light blue 5512, and light purple 5231.

NEEDLES: US 9 (5.5mm).

GAUGE: 17 sts x 20 rows = 4 x 4in (10 x 10 cm).

 ─────────────────────────

Make one chick in each of white, light blue, and light purple.

HEART: Cast on and knit Regular heart (see p. 9). Fill the heart with wadding and sew up any gaps.

FEET: Cut out 2 feet (see p. 125 for template) in orange or apricot rubber. Glue them to the chicks using a glue gun. For extra support, cut short lengths of metal wire and glue them under each foot.

HEAD: Cut out the beak (see p. 125 for template) in orange rubber. Fold it in half on the dotted line, and attach it to the front of the chicks with a few stitches on each side. Make a couple of stitches through the whole beak in the middle, at the base of the beak, so the top and bottom parts of the beak stay together. Attach the eyes above the beak.

WINGS: Attach fake fur or feathers on each side of the chick for the wings.

YOU'LL NEVER LOSE ANYTHING AGAIN! WITH COLORFUL HEART
PENDANTS, KEYS AND CELL PHONES ARE MUCH EASIER TO FIND.

PERSONAL PENDANTS

KEY PENDANT

HEART MEASUREMENTS: Width 3in (8cm), height
4¾in (12cm).

MATERIALS:

- Wadding
- Small spring hook
- Wooden letters 1¾in (4.5cm) high
- Orange acrylic paint
- Yellow relief paint
- Glue (glue gun)

YARN: Lambswool yarn (100% wool, 50g =
273yd/250m), 50g in each of pink L56 and red L43.

NEEDLES: US 0 (2mm), plus B1 (2mm) crochet
hook.

GAUGE: 30 sts x 46 rows = 4 x 4in (10 x 10cm).

♥ ————————————————————

HEART: Cast on using the top colors on
the charts below, and knit Long heart (see
p. 9). After increasing up to 10 sts, knit the
color pattern following the charts below. Fill
the finished heart with wadding, and sew
together any gaps.

EMBRODERY: Embroider knot stitches
evenly spaced over the heart using the yarn
held double; use pink on red and red on
pink.

LOOP: Crochet a chain in the desired color
and length, and crochet 1 sl st in each ch.
Fold the chain to form a loop and sew to
the dip of the heart. Attach the heart to the
spring hook.

LETTERS: Paint the wooden letters orange
and let them dry. Apply as many coats as
necessary. Paint on yellow dots and let to
dry. Glue one letter onto each heart.

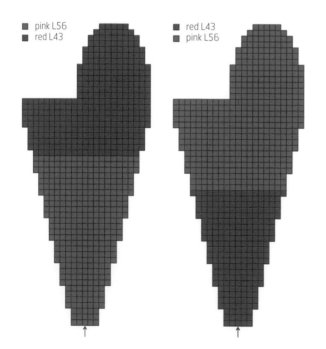

■ pink L56
■ red L43

■ red L43
■ pink L56

*If you decorate your hearts with your own
initials everyone will know who the lucky
owner of the keys is.*

60

Not everyone has orange buttons lying around. Use the buttons you have and choose the color of the heart accordingly, or buy a bag of assorted buttons from a craft store.

CELL PHONE PENDANT

HEART MEASUREMENTS: Width 2½in (6.5cm), height 3½in (9cm).

MATERIALS:
• Wadding
• Assorted buttons
• Gold thread
• Extra-strong sewing thread in coordinating color

YARN: Plum (70% mohair, 30% polyamide, 25g = 273yd/250m), 25g orange 025; Metallic (45% polyamide, 55% metallic thread, 1 bobbin = 1093yd/1000m), 1 bobbin copper 327.

NEEDLES: US 0 (2mm), plus B1 (2mm) crochet hook.

GAUGE: 38 sts x 60 rows with one strand each of Plum and Metallic = 4 x 4in (10 x 10cm).

♥ —————————————————————

HEART: Cast on with one strand of each yarn and knit the Long heart (see p. 9).

Fill the finished heart with wadding, and sew up any gaps.

EMBELLISHMENTS: Sew the buttons to the heart with the gold thread.

LOOP: Using the extra-strong sewing thread, crochet a 5½in (14cm)-long chain; you can either use the crochet hook or you can finger-crochet. Fold the chain into a loop and sew it to the pit of the heart. If you only use small sts in the pit, they can easily come loose. Therefore, sew some long stitches through to the tip of the heart so the loop is better secured.

PENGUINS

PENGUINS

HEART MEASUREMENTS: Width 4in (10cm), height 6in (15cm).

MATERIALS:
- Wadding
- White buttons (for eyes)
- Acrylic paint or paint pen in orange, blue, red, brown, and black
- Wooden feet
- Skis and ski poles
- Toy sled
- White Fimo soft clay
- Glue (glue gun)

YARN: Petunia (100% cotton, 50g = 120yd/110m), 100g black 297, 50g in each of white 296 and orange 278.

NEEDLES: US 2/3 (3mm).

GAUGE: 24 sts x 36 rows = 4 x 4in (10 x 10cm).

♥ ————————————————————————

Make three penguins.

BODY: Cast on with orange yarn and knit the Long heart (see p. 9). After 7 rows, switch to black and finish the heart in this color. Fill the finished heart with wadding, and sew up any gaps. Fold the bottom 1½in (4cm) upward and sew down to make the head. Draw black pupils on the two white buttons and attach where the beak and body meet to make the eyes.

TUMMY: Using the white yarn, cast on 5 sts. Work in st st back and forth, and inc on each side on every other needle: 2 sts once, 1 st two times (13 sts). Knit till the piece measures 2½in (6cm). Bind off 1 st on each side on every other needle: 1 st two times, 2 sts once (5 sts). Bind off. Sew the tummy onto the penguin.

WINGS: Using black yarn, cast on 3 sts. Work in st st back and forth. On three needles, cast off 1 st on each side. Rep this step on every fourth needle until you have 9 sts. Knit till the piece measures 4in (10cm). Bind off 1 st on each side on every needle till 3 sts rem. After last bind-off, knit on two needles. Bind off. Rep for the other wing. Sew the wings onto the penguin, one on each side at shoulder height.

FEET: Paint the feet orange and glue to the penguin.

WINTER ACTIVITY EQUIPMENT: Paint the sled green, the skis blue, and the ski poles red and brown. Make a snow lantern and a simple snowball of Fimo clay, and bake in an oven on 110°C for 10–30 minutes. The snow lantern can stand separately; the rest of the equipment is glued onto the penguins.

Don't these charming little athletes warm your heart?

SARA LIVES HERE! IT CAN BE
FUN TO HAVE YOUR NAME ON
THE DOOR TO YOUR ROOM.

THE DOOR TO YOUR HEART

NAMETAGS S-A-R-A

HEART MEASUREMENTS: Width 3in (7.5cm),
height 3¾in (9.5cm).

MATERIALS:
- Wadding
- Wooden letters, 2in (5cm) high
- Orange, yellow, and red acrylic paint
- 2 small yellow buttons
- 2 screws (for hanging)
- Glue (glue gun)

YARN: Inca (100% alpaca, 50g = 191yd/175m),
50g in each of green 739, apple green 006, light
turquoise 705, and turquoise 008. Use leftovers or
50g in each of red 733, orange 250, and yellow 007.

NEEDLES: US 0 (2mm) plus C2/D3 (3mm) crochet
hook.

GAUGE: 32 sts x 46 rows = 4 x 4in (10 x 10cm).

♥ ————————————————————————

HEARTS: Knit 1 Regular heart in each of
green, apple green, light turquoise, and
turquoise (see p. 9). Fill the finished hearts
with wadding, and sew up any gaps.

EMBROIDERY: Using the yarn held double,
embroider yellow knot stitches spaced
evenly over the light turquoise and
turquoise hearts.

2 CROCHET CIRCLES: Use the yarn held
double. For one circle use the color before
the parentheses; for the second use the
color inside the parentheses. Cast on with
orange[red].

Join 6 ch in a circle with 1 sl st.

Row 1: Crochet 10 sc in the circle.

Row 2: Switch to red[orange]. Crochet 2 dc
in each sc (20 dc). 1 dc is replaced with 2 ch,
and the row ends with 1 sl st in the top of 1
dc.

Row 3: Switch to apple green[light
turquoise]. Crochet 1 sc in each dc, then 2 sc
in each 4 dc (25 sc).

FLOWERS: Use a single strand of orange
yarn. Make a loose loop. Crochet (6 ch + 1 sl
st) five times in the loop. Tighten the loop,
and tie together the threads. Attach a button
in the middle of the flower.

Crochet a similar flower in red.

If the name you want to make has more than four letters, make more hearts described, or use new colors as you wish.

STRING: Use the orange yarn held double. Crochet a chain-stitch string to the desired length. Switch to a single strand of red yarn. Turn and crochet 1 sl st in each ch.

LETTERS: Paint the letters orange and let them dry. Paint yellow dots with a red center on one (or more) of the letters; paint red dots with a yellow center on another (or more).

TO FINISH: Lay the hearts (with letters on top) in the desired order, and make any necessary adjustments. When you are happy with the result, use a crochet hook to pull the string through the hearts. Put the crochet hook sideways through the heart and pull the string (the end that doesn't have a knot) back through the heart; it doesn't matter if the hearts are a little tilted and hang differently on the string. Sew each end to a crochet circle. Glue the letters to the hearts.

HANGING: Hang the name tag using a screw in the middle of each crochet circle. Glue a flower on top of each screw knob – the color on the flower should be the same as the one in the middle of the crochet circle.

Love hearts

A HEART OF GOLD

BROCADE HEART

HEART MEASUREMENTS: Width 3½in (8.5cm), height 15¼in (13.5cm).

MATERIALS:
- 1 spool of gold string
- Pearls
- Chain, antique copper
- Touch Textile Metal, Yellow Gold

NEEDLES: US 2/3 (3mm).

GAUGE: 28 sts x 40 rows = 4 x 4in (10 x 10cm).

♥ ——————————————————————

HEART: Cast on with gold string and knit the Long heart (see p. 9).

EMBELLISHMENT: Draw brocade pattern with Touch Textile Metal on the front of the heart, and place the pearls in the paint while it is still wet. Leave to dry.

TO FINISH: Sew the chain to the back of the heart. Sew pearls to the chain.

GOLD HEART WITH THREE CHAINS

HEART MEASUREMENTS: Width 2¾in (7cm), height 3¼in (8cm).

MATERIALS:
- Wadding
- 1 silver ball chain
- 1 silver chain 5mm
- 1 silver chain 2.5mm
- 1 pearl for embellishment

YARN: Concorde (64% viscose, 36% polyester), 25g gold 20.

NEEDLES: US ½ (2.5mm).

GAUGE: 35 sts x 53 rows = 4 x 4in (10 x 10cm).

♥ ——————————————————————

HEART: Cast on and knit Regular heart (see p. 9).

Fill the finished heart with wadding, and sew up any gaps.

TO FINISH: Sew the chains to the back of the heart and the pearl to the dip in the front.

Some yarn, a free night, a length of chain, and some extra embellishments – you don't need anything else if you want to make a personal and unique gold necklace.

Heart's choice

GURO
(photographer):
My favorite heart is this necklace. The heart is the most beautiful symbol there is. This heart is soft and light, just how a heart should be. It is both nostalgic and feminine, perfect for either casual wear or for dressing up.

THESE HEARTS ARE KNITTED IN THE SOFTEST ALPACA YARN YOU CAN FIND. A HINT OF GOLD GIVES A WONDERFUL FEELING OF LUXURY.

SOFT LOVE

LARGE HEART PILLOW

HEART MEASUREMENTS: Width 17¼in (44cm), height 21¼in (54cm).

MATERIALS:
- Wadding
- Beige teddy bear fabric

YARN: Puno Metallic (58% alpaca, 10% merino, 13% polyamide, 19% polyester, 50g = 120yd/110m), 250g gold 30314; Concorde (64% viscose, 36% polyester), 25g gold 20.

NEEDLES: US 36 (20mm), plus size 7 (4.5mm) crochet hook.

GAUGE: 5.5 sts x 8 rows with four strands of Puno held together = 4 x 4in (10 x 10cm).

♥ ────────────────────────────

HEART: Cast on with four strands of Puno yarn held together, and knit Regular heart (see p. 9). Fill the finished heart with wadding, and sew up any gaps.

FUR EDGE: Cut a piece of the teddy bear fabric about 2in (5cm) in width and as long as the outline of the heart. Sew it to the heart.

LETTERS: Use four strands of Concorde yarn held together.

Crochet a chain about 59in (150cm) long, turn, and place 1 sl st in each ch. Form letters (see p. 125 for template for "Hope" lettering; shown there half-size) and sew these to the pillow.

 Baste the stitches of the letters before you attach the gold string. It will be easier to make the lettering look good and to measure the exact length of the string.

TWO SMALL HANGING HEARTS

HEART MEASUREMENTS: Width 8¾in (22cm), height 9½in (24cm).

MATERIALS:
• Wadding
• Some leftover teddy bear fabric
• 2 large buttons
• a small piece of cardboard about 4in (10cm) in width

YARN (FOR BOTH HEARTS): Puno (68% alpaca, 22% polyamide, 10% merino, 50g = 120yd/110m), 50g in each of natural 811 and beige 1314; Concorde (64% viscose, 36% polyester), 75g gold 20.

NEEDLES: US 13 (9mm), plus size 7 (4.5mm) and N/P15 (10mm) crochet hooks.

GAUGE: 10 sts x 18 rows with Puno yarn held double = 4 x 4in (10 x 10cm).

♥ ————————————————————————

Knit one heart in beige and one in natural.

HEART: Cast on with yarn held double and knit the Regular heart (see p. 9). Fill the finished heart with wadding, and sew up any gaps.

EDGING: Use eight strands of the gold yarn held together and N/P15 (10mm) crochet hook.

Crochet a chain the length of the heart outline and sew it to the heart.

HANGING STRING: Use four strands of the gold yarn held together and size 7 (4.5mm) crochet hook.

Crochet a chain to the desired length, turn, and make 1 sl st in each ch. Fold the string double to make a loop, make a seam at the end, and sew the loop to the pit of the heart.

TASSEL: Coil the remainder of the gold yarn around the cardboard to make two tassels the same size to attach to the tips of the hearts. NB: Do not cut the fringes of the tassels, or the yarn will run.

BUTTON EMBELLISHMENT: Sew a button to the middle of the heart. If you want to, put teddy bear fabric around the button (as shown here on the beige heart).

I like mixing together different kinds of textures and materials. Here I used fur, wool, and metallic thread all blended together. Lovely!

LOVE IS IN THE AIR

PRISM HEARTS

HEART MEASUREMENTS:
Regular white hearts: Width 2½in (6.5cm), height 2¾in (7cm).
Long white hearts: Width 2½in (6.5cm), height 3½in (9cm).
Regular silver heart: Width 2¾in (7cm), height 3in (8cm).
Long silver heart: Width 2¾in (7cm), height 4in (10cm).

MATERIALS:
• Wadding
• 4 "icicles," length 2in (50mm)
• 2 "drops," length 1½in (38mm)
• 6 balls, diameter ½in (12mm)
• 6 balls, diameter ¾in (19mm)
• 2 ovals, length 2in (50mm)
• 4 stars, 1½in (40mm)
• 13 prisms, diameter ⅜in (11mm)
• Various pearls

YARN: Plum (70% mohair, 30% polyamide, 25g = 273yd/250m), 25g white 00; Metallic (45% polyamide, 55% metallic fiber, 1 bobbin = 1093yd/1000m), 1 bobbin silver 342; Concorde (64% viscose, 36% polyester), 25g silver 21.

NEEDLES: US 0 (2mm) (for white hearts) and ½ (2.5mm) (for silver hearts), plus B1 (2mm) crochet hook.

GAUGE FOR WHITE HEARTS: 38 sts x 60 rows with 1 strand each of Plum and Metallic = 4 x 4in (10 x 10cm).

GAUGE FOR SILVER HEARTS: 35 sts x 53 rows with single strand of Concorde = 4 x 4in (10 x 10cm).

♥ ─────────────────────────────

WHITE HEARTS: Use size 0 (2mm) needles and one strand each of Plum and Metallic. Knit five Rormal hearts and four Long hearts (see p. 9). Fill the finished hearts with wadding, and sew together any gaps. Decorate with pearls and prisms.

SILVER HEARTS: Use size 1/2 (2.5mm) needles and single strand of Concorde. Knit three Regular hearts and three Long hearts (see p. 9). Fill the finished hearts with wadding, and sew up any gaps. Decorate with pearls and prisms, making sure you have one prism (= 1 button) left over for each string.

Here you can see an overload of pearls and prisms that look great used together. The secret is to use colors that give an overall impression with colors that coordinate.

STRING: Use Concorde yarn. Crochet chain to the desired length (remember to leave extra for whatever you attach the string to), turn, and make one sl st in each ch. Finish off with a few extra inches of chain, which will be turned into a loop (should be able to fit the prisms). Attach one prism (= 1 button) in desired length to the loop so that the string fits the pendant it will be attached to.

TO FINISH: Put hearts, prisms, and pearls on the string in the desired order – use the photographs as a guide or make your own pattern. Make any necessary adjustments. When you are happy with the result, pull the string through each piece: start with the piece on top, then work your way down. Use the crochet hook when pulling the string through the hearts; insert it from the bottom and pull the string back through the heart. See the Tip for how to pull the string through the pearls and prisms. Sew on prisms and pearls to the string ends.

Tip

- How does a camel pass through the eye of a needle? And how do you get a thick string through a small hole? In this case I used strong thread (you could also use dental floss) to get the crochet silver thread through the big circular balls. Take a needle with the thread through the ball, through the end of the string, and then back through the ball. Remove the needle and pull in both threads so you can get the string through the hole.

- The pendants can be hung used in all sorts of ways; for example, hang them in the window. Or get a rough branch, decorate with the pendants, and hang it as a beautiful arrangement above the dining-room table.

THESE HEARTS ARE TIED TOGETHER – A NICE ROMANTIC GESTURE.
B IS FOR BENTE AND M IS FOR MORTEN.

PAIR OF HEARTS

PAIR OF HEARTS

STOCKINETTE HEART MEASUREMENTS: Width 5in (13cm), height 8¼in (21cm).

SEED STITCH HEART MEASUREMENTS: Width 5½in (14cm), height 7½in (19cm).

MATERIALS:
- Wadding
- White sateen string
- Fabric letters
- Ribbon for hanging loops

YARN (FOR BOTH HEARTS): Sumatra (100% cotton, 50g = 93yd/85m), 100g white 3003.

NEEDLES: US 7 (4.5mm), plus E4 (3.5mm) crochet hook.

GAUGE: 19 sts x 25 rows for st st heart; 17 sts x 28 rows for seed stitch heart = 4 x 4in (10 x 10cm).

♥ ─────────────────────────

Knit one heart in st st and one in seed stitch.

HEART: Cast on and knit Long heart (see p. 9). Seed stitch heart only: After increasing to 10 sts, follow chart right for stitch pattern.

Fill the finished hearts with wadding, and sew up any gaps.

CROCHET EDGING OF STOCKINETTE HEART:

Row 1: Fasten the thread with 1 sc in the edge (stick down 2 around 2 sts on the side). *Crochet 2 ch, skip about ⅜in (1cm) at the edge, 1 sc at the edge*, rep from * to *, but in the pit of the heart leave the 2 ch. At the end of the row, replace 1 last sc with 1 ch in the first st.

Row 2: Crochet 2 sc in each 2 ch. Close row with 1 sl st in first st.

CROCHET EDGING OF SEED STITCH HEART:

Row 1: Same as for st st heart.

Row 2: Crochet 1 sl st + 3 ch + 1 sl st in each ch.

LETTERS: Attach the fabric letters to the front of the hearts or make your own letters with sateen string: double over the string and sew together. Shape to form letters and attach to heart.

HANGING LOOP: Sew ribbon to the heart for hanging loop; here, the same ribbon was used for both hearts.

□ knit
▣ purl

Not the same, but similar!
B is made in seed stitch
with a lace edging, while M
is in stockinette edged with
a simple crochet border.
You can make the letters or
buy them ready-made.

CRAFTED PLACE CARDS MAKE SPECIAL OCCASIONS EVEN MORE
PERSONAL. IT'S NICE TO TREAT THE ONE YOU LOVE.

HAPPY ANNIVERSARY!

PLACE CARDS

HEART MEASUREMENTS: Width 2½in (6cm), height 3½in (8.5cm).

MATERIALS:
- Wadding
- White and/or silver ribbon
- Place card foot
- Clear plastic sheets
- Waterproof pen/felt pen, silver or white, or stick-on letters
- Pin
- 2 silver pearls (with holes big enough for the pin)
- Glue (glue gun)

YARN: Plum (70% mohair, 30% polyamide, 25g = 273yd/250m), 25g white 001 and/or light gray 057.

NEEDLES: US 0 (2mm).

GAUGE: 40 sts x 62 rows = 4 x 4in (10 x 10cm).

 ————————————————————

WHITE PLACE CARD

HEART: Cast on with white yarn and knit Long heart (see p. 9). Fill the finished heart with wadding, and sew up any gaps.

TO FINISH: Attach the heart to the place card foot.

EMBELLISHMENT: Make a white bow, leaving the ends are long. Sew the curve onto the heart on one of the sides.

NAME TAG: Write or place stick-on letters on the plastic (see Tip), and cut out an oval shape. Thread a silver pearl onto the pin and glue. Attach the name tag to the heart with the needle.

 ————————————————————

GRAY PLACE CARD

HEART: Cast on with gray yarn and knit Long heart (see p. 9). Fill the finished heart with wadding, and sew up any gaps.

TO FINISH: Attach the heart to the place card foot.

EMBELLISHMENT: Make a silver bow around the place card foot, right under the heart.

NAME TAG: Write or place stick-on letters on the plastic (see Tip), and cut out a rectangular shape. Thread a silver pearl onto the pin and glue. Attach the name tag to the heart with the needle.

Tip If you have trouble making the letters look nice, find a font you like on the computer and print out the name you need. Place it under the plastic sheet and then trace over it.

*Happy anniversary!
There's no question who
we are celebrating here.*

LOVE FROM

TURQUOISE HEART MESSAGE

HEART MEASUREMENTS: Width 2½in (6.5cm), height 3½in (9cm).

MATERIALS:
- Wadding
- Pearls
- Transparent thread
- White ribbon
- Silver cardboard
- Clear plastic sheet
- White waterproof pen

YARN: Plum (70% mohair, 30% polyamide, 25g = 273yd/250m), leftovers or 25g turquoise 077; Metallic (45% polyamide, 55% metallic fiber, 1 bobbin = 1093yd/1000m), 1 bobbin turquoise 365.

NEEDLES: US 0 (2mm).

GAUGE: 38 sts x 60 rows with 1 strand each of Plum and Metallic = 4 x 4in (10 x 10cm).

♥ ─────────────────────────────────

HEART: Cast on with one strand of each type and knit the Long heart (see p. 9).

Fill the finished heart with wadding, and sew up any gaps.

EMBELLISHMENTS: Sew pearls onto the front side of the heart using the transparent thread.

CARD: Cut out a rectangle in both cardboard and plastic. Write the required name on the plastic. Put the two rectangles on top of each other and make a hole.

TO FINISH: Make a loop in ribbon and attach it to the pit of the heart. When wrapping the gift, thread the ribbon through the loop in the heart and the hole in the card.

While the wrapping and card might be thrown away, the heart can be reused. Add a pin or magnet that can be attached to the back.

WHITE HEART MESSAGE

HEART MEASUREMENTS: Width 2½in (6.5cm), height 3½in (9cm).

MATERIALS:
- Wadding
- Silver glitter glue
- Scrapbooking paper and/or cardboard
- White ribbon
- Clear plastic sheet
- Silver letter stickers
- Glue

YARN: Plum (70% mohair, 30% polyamide, 25g = 273yd/250m), leftovers or 25g white 001.

NEEDLES: US 0 (2mm).

GAUGE: 38 sts x 60 rows = 4 x 4in (10 x 10cm).

♥ ─────────────────────────────

HEART: Cast on and knit the Long heart (see p. 9). Fill the finished heart with wadding, and sew up any gaps.

EMBELLISHMENTS: Draw a brocade pattern with the glitter glue on the front of the heart.

CARD: Cut the card (here 4 x 8¼in/10.5 x 21cm) from scrapbooking paper and/or cardboard. Put the parts on top of each other, make a hole in one corner, and attach with ribbon. Cut out a small rectangle in plastic (here 4 x 1½in/10.5 x 4cm), glue letters to the plastic, and attach the plastic to the card.

TO FINISH: Attach the heart to the card – you can either use glue or sew the heart on. If you sew the heart on, the receiver can simply remove the stitches and reuse the heart later.

MAKE ONE OF THESE BEAUTIFUL NECKLACES; ONE HEART HAS THE
BEADS INSIDE, THE OTHER HAS BEADS ATTACHED TO IT.

HEART TO HEART

BEAD-FILLED METAL HEART

HEART MEASUREMENTS: Width 3½in (9cm),
height 4in (10cm).

MATERIALS:
- Metal crochet thread, silver, 0.18 mm
- 1 bag crackled glass beads, diam. ½in (8mm),
  mixed colors
- 1 neck ring
- Transparent thread

NEEDLES: US 0 (2mm).

GAUGE: 27 sts x 53 rows = 4 x 4in (10 x 10cm).

♥ ————————————————

HEART: Cast on with metal thread and knit
the Long heart (see p. 9).

BEAD FILLING: Fill the finished heart
with beads. Sew up and down with the
transparent thread across the whole heart
so the beads stay in place – when you pick
up the heart, the beads should not all fall to
the bottom.

TO FINISH: Thread the heart onto the neck
ring along with some extra beads.

BEADED HEART

HEART MEASUREMENTS: Width 2½in (6.5cm),
height 3in (7.5cm).

MATERIALS:
- Wadding
- 1 box faced transparent beads, mixed sizes
- 1 neck ring
- Transparent thread

YARN: Plum (70% mohair, 30% polyamide, 25g =
273yd/250m), leftovers or 25g white 001; Metallic
(45% polyamide, 55% metallic fiber, 1 bobbin =
1093yd/1000m), 1 bobbin silver 342.

NEEDLES: US 0 (2mm).

GAUGE: 38 sts x 60 rows with 1 strand of each yarn
held together = 4 x 4in (10 x 10cm).

♥ ————————————————

HEART: Cast on with one strand of each
yarn. Knit Regular heart (see p. 9). Fill the
heart with wadding, and sew up any gaps.

EMBELLISHMENT: Sew beads onto the front
of the heart using transparent thread.

TO FINISH: Thread heart onto neck ring.

 Knitting with metal thread can
be hard because of its lack of
elasticity. This one is also thin
and may break easily. However,
the ends can be reattached by
twisting them together.

 If you want an even outline for
the heart, start by sewing a row
of same-sized beads along the
edge. Then fill the heart with
mixed-sized beads.

The hearts can easily be taken on and off the neck ring. If you attach a brooch pin to the back of the heart, you could also use it on a bag, dress, or belt.

WONDERFUL SOFT BOUCLÉ PILLOWS ARE PERFECT TO
CUDDLE UP WITH AFTER A LONG DAY, ALONG WITH A
GOOD CUP OF COFFEE. OR MAYBE YOU PREFER TEA?

I LOVE COFFEE,
I LOVE TEA

I LOVE COFFEE ...

HEART MEASUREMENTS: Width 15in (38cm),
height 17¾in (45cm).

MATERIALS:
• Wadding
• Off-white textured fabric (felt or fleece)
• Pink and brown embroidery thread

YARN: Dale Monjita (91% alpaca, 7.5% wool, 1.5%
nylon, 100g = 98yd/90m), 200g light gray 0004.

NEEDLES: US 17 (12mm).

GAUGE: 6.5 sts x 9.5 rows with yarn held double = 4
x 4in (10 x 10cm).

♥ ────────────────────────

HEART: Cast on with yarn held double and
knit the Regular heart (see p. 9). Fill the
finished heart with wadding, and sew up
any gaps.

EMBELLISHMENT: Cut a fabric rectangle
3 x 9½in (8 x 24cm). Embroider in pink
(see p. 124) using contour stitches. Sew the
rectangle to the front using double thread in
brown and tack just inside the edge.

I LOVE TEA ...

HEART MEASUREMENTS: Width 15in (38cm),
height 17¾in (45cm).

MATERIALS:
• Wadding
• Brown and pink run-textured fabric (felt or fleece)
• White and brown embroidery thread

YARN: Dale Monjita (91% alpaca, 7.5% wool, 1.5%
nylon, 100g = 98yd/90m), 200g off-white 0010.

NEEDLES: US 17 (12mm).

GAUGE: 6.5 sts x 9.5 rows with yarn held double = 4
x 4in (10 x 10cm).

♥ ────────────────────────

HEART: Cast on with yarn held double and
knit the Regular heart (see p. 9). Fill the
finished heart with wadding, and sew up
any gaps.

EMBELLISHMENT: Cut out text and small
hearts (see p. 124) from fabric. Attach the
pieces to the front (use picture as guide); use
double thread in brown and tack just inside
the edge.

Heart's choice

MORTEN
(dearest partner and husband):

*This one is my favorite! I like the
colors, I love coffee, and it makes me
want to lay my head on it – it's really
nice and soft.*

The hearts are knitted with the yarn held double and produce a nice big pillow. If you want to make them even bigger, you can experiment by using chunkier yarn on thicker needles.

Winter hearts

DECEMBER IS THE TIME FOR WAITING. WE LIGHT
CANDLES AND PREPARE FOR CHRISTMAS.

HEARTS THAT WAIT

ADVENT HEARTS

HEART MEASUREMENTS: Width 3½in (9cm),
height 4½in (11cm).

MATERIALS:
- Wadding
- Ribbon or string for hanging
- Advent numbers

YARN: Pt2 (100% wool, 50g = 180yd/165m), 50g in
each of purple 43, deep purple 42, blue-purple 41,
and red-purple 46; Concorde (64% viscose, 36%
polyester), 25g silver 21.

NEEDLES: US 2/3 (3mm).

GAUGE: 27 sts x 40 rows = 4 x 4in (10 x 10cm).

♥ ──────────────────────────────

FIRST SUNDAY OF ADVENT

HEART: Cast on with purple yarn, and knit
the Regular heart (see p. 9). After increasing
to 10 sts, knit color pattern following chart
below. Fill the finished heart with wadding,
and sew up any gaps.

TO FINISH: Sew ribbon to the heart for
hanging and the number 1 in the middle
between the curves of the heart.

♥ ──────────────────────────────

SECOND SUNDAY OF ADVENT

HEART: Cast on with deep purple yarn, and
knit the Regular heart (see p. 9). Fill the
finished heart with wadding, and sew up
any gaps.

EMBELLISHMENT: Embroider a snowflake
in the middle of the heart (use the
illustration as a guide) using the silver yarn
held double.

TO FINISH: Sew ribbon to the heart for
hanging and the number 2 in the middle
between the curves of the heart.

♥ ──────────────────────────────

THIRD SUNDAY OF ADVENT

HEART: Cast on with blue-purple yarn,
and knit the Regular heart (see p. 9). After
increasing to 10 sts, knit color pattern
following chart below. Fill the finished heart
with wadding, and sew up any gaps.

TO FINISH: Sew ribbon to the heart for
hanging and the number 3 in the middle
between the curves of the heart.

♥ ──────────────────────────────

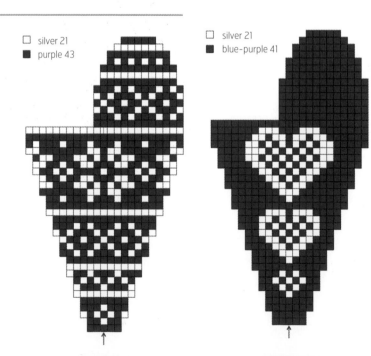

☐ silver 21
■ purple 43

☐ silver 21
■ blue-purple 41

All the hearts are made in different shades of purple and feature different patterns and embellishments. Follow the patterns to make them exactly like those pictured, or make up your own.

FOURTH SUNDAY OF ADVENT

HEART: Cast on with red-purple yarn, and knit the Regular heart (see p. 9). Fill the finished heart with wadding, and sew up any gaps.

EMBELLISHMENT: Embroider different sized crosses all over the heart with knot stitches in the middle of each cross – use a single strand of silver thread.

TO FINISH: Sew ribbon to the heart for hanging and the number 4 in the middle between the curves of the heart.

 Tip
It's not unusual to knit a little tighter in gauge when knitting a pattern in two colors. The finished hearts can therefore end up being a little different in width. To avoid this you can switch to thicker needles when you follow the color pattern.

If the patterned hearts are still a bit too wide, sew a few stitches across on the inside to make them narrower.

CHRISTMAS IN MY HEART

CALENDAR HEARTS

HEART MEASUREMENTS: Width 3½in (9cm), height 4½in (11.5cm).

MATERIALS:
- Wadding
- Wooden numbers 1¾in (4.5cm)
- White, orange, and pink acrylic paint
- Buttons
- Glue (glue gun)
- Natural-colored string
- Hooks for hanging

YARN: Fine wool (100% wool, 50g = 191yd/175m), 50g in each of white 400, red 418, and deep red 435, plus leftovers or 50g orange 4205 and pink 4686.

NEEDLES: US 2/3 (3mm).

GAUGE: 26 sts x 37 rows with pattern = 4 x 4in (10 x 10cm).

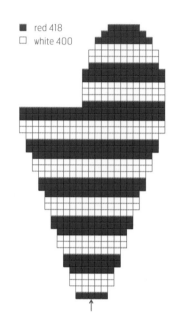

red 418
white 400

DECEMBER 1ST

HEART: Cast on with red yarn, and knit the Regular heart (see p. 9). Fill the finished heart with wadding, and sew up any gaps.

EMBELLISHMENTS: Baste-stitch a pink seam right on the inside of the contour on the front side of the heart using yarn held double. Sew a button in the middle of the heart using yarn that contrasts with the color of the button, and tie it (rather than attaching it). Cut the threads so they end up being approx. ⅜in (1cm). Paint the number 1 white and let it dry. Glue a piece of white yarn to the number and attach the yarn between the curves of the heart.

♥ ─────────────────────

DECEMBER 2ND

HEART: Cast on with deep red yarn, and knit the Regular heart (see p. 9). Fill the finished heart with wadding, and sew up any gaps.

EMBELLISHMENTS: Embroider pink knot stitches randomly over the heart using yarn held double. Paint the number 2 orange, let it dry, then glue to middle of heart.

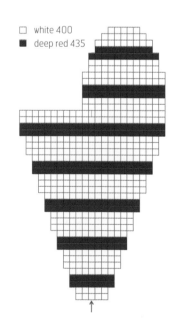

white 400
deep red 435

You don't need to knit 24
hearts! Make as many as
you would like. For Advent
days without hearts,
maybe hang up little gifts
or greeting cards instead.

DECEMBER 3RD

HEART: Cast on with red yarn, and knit the Regular heart (see p. 9). After increasing to 10 sts, knit color pattern following top chart on p. 92. Fill the finished heart with wadding, and sew up any gaps.

EMBELLISHMENTS: Sew a button in the middle of the heart; use a colored thread that contrasts with the color of the button, and tie it (rather than attaching it). Cut the threads so they end up about ⅜in (1cm).

Paint the number 3 pink, and let it dry. Glue white yarn to the number and attach the yarn between the curves of the heart.

♥ ————————————————————

DECEMBER 4TH

HEART: Cast on with red yarn, and knit the Regular heart (see p. 9). Fill the finished heart with wadding, and sew up any gaps.

EMBELLISHMENTS: Sew two buttons in the middle of the heart. Use colored thread that with contrasts the color of the button, and tie it rather than attaching it. Cut the threads so they end up about ⅜in (1cm).

Paint the number 4 white, and let it dry. Glue white yarn to the number and attach it between the curves of the heart.

♥ ————————————————————

DECEMBER 5TH

HEART: Cast on with white yarn, and knit the Regular heart (see p. 9). Fill the finished heart with wadding, and sew up any gaps.

EMBELLISHMENTS: Baste-stitch a deep red seam right on the inside of the contour on the front side of the heart using yarn held double. Paint the number 5 pink and let it dry. Glue the number to the middle of the heart.

♥ ————————————————————

DECEMBER 6TH

HEART: Cast on with deep red yarn, and knit the Regular heart (see p. 9). Fill the finished heart with wadding, and sew up any gaps.

EMBELLISHMENTS: Embroider orange knot stitches randomly across the heart using yarn held double. Paint the number 6 white and let it dry. Glue the number to the middle of the heart.

♥ ————————————————————

DECEMBER 7TH

HEART: Cast on with white yarn, and knit the Regular heart (see p. 9). After increasing to 10 sts, knit color pattern following lower chart on p. 92. Fill the finished heart with wadding, and sew up any gaps.

EMBELLISHMENTS: Tack-stitch pink seams on every other white stripe using yarn held double. Paint the number 7 orange and let it dry. Glue the number to the middle of the heart.

♥ ————————————————————

DECEMBER 8–24

HEART: Knit hearts from your own imagination or repeat one of the already described hearts.

♥ ————————————————————

TO FINISH: Twist double natural-colored string (= quadruple strands). Lay the hearts out in desired order and adjust as necessary. When you are happy with the effect, use a crochet hook to pull the string through the hearts: Insert the hook sideways through the heart and pull the string (in the end without a knot) back through the heart.

HANGING: Attach hooks and hang up the Advent hearts.

 One heart requires about 6.5g yarn, so with one 50g ball of thread you can make seven hearts. 200g of yarn should therefore be enough for 24 hearts.

CHRISTMAS ISN'T CHRISTMAS WITHOUT SANTA! THESE CHARMING
FELLOWS ARE MADE FROM UPSIDE-DOWN HEARTS.

HEART SANTAS

2 SANTAS

HEART MEASUREMENTS: Width 4in (10.5cm),
height 6¾in (17cm).

MATERIALS:
- Wadding
- White and gray curly doll hair
- 2 big beads
- Plastic eyes, diameter ⅜in (1cm)
- White yarn
- White felt
- Glue (glue gun)

YARN (BOTH SANTAS): Mitu (50% alpaca, 50%
wool, 50g = 109yd/100m), 50 red 0042.

NEEDLES: US 4 (3.5mm).

GAUGE: 23 sts x 31 rows = 4x 4in (10 x 10cm).

♥ ————————————————————

HEART: Cast on and knit the Long heart (see
p. 9). Fill the finished heart with wadding,
and sew up any gaps.

EMBELLISHMENTS: Cut a piece of felt
2½ x 9½in (6 x 24cm). Fold ½in (1.5cm) to
the wrong side on the long sides, put the
short sides together, wrong side to wrong
side, and sew a seam (with ⅜in/1cm seam
allowance) for the hat brim. Thread the
brim downward over the hat (= upside-
down heart), and mark by the edge. Attach
the beard below the brim. Attach the brim,
nose (1 bead), and eyes.

Make a white tassel and attach it to the top
of the hat, together with string for hanging.

A red heart is turned upside down. Add hat, beard, bead nose, eyes, and a tassel – suddenly you have a finished Santa.

DECORATE YOUR CHRISTMAS TREE WITH LOVELY HEARTS
IN RED AND WHITE. THEY ARE FAIRLY LARGE SO YOU WON'T
NEED MANY HEARTS TO DECORATE A SMALL TREE.

YULETIDE HEARTS

SIX CHRISTMAS TREE HEARTS

HEART MEASUREMENTS: Width 3½in (9cm), height 5½in (14cm).

MATERIALS:
• Wadding
• Natural-colored string

YARN: Fine wool (100% wool, 50g = 191yd/175m), 50g in each of white 400 and deep red 435.

NEEDLES: US 2/3 (3mm).

GAUGE: 27 sts x 38 rows with pattern = 4 x 4in (10 x 10cm).

♥ ————————————————————————

HEARTS: Cast on with the top color on the chart of your choice (see pp. 100–101), and knit the Long heart (see p. 9). After increasing to 10 sts, knit the color pattern according to the charts overleaf. Fill the finished heart with wadding, and sew up any gaps.

TO FINISH: Attach string for hanging.

Here we offer ideas for six different hearts, but you could also experiment with making your own patterns!

■ deep red 435
□ white 400

■ deep red 435
□ white 400

■ deep red 435
□ white 400

□ white 400
■ deep red 435

□ white 400
■ deep red 435

□ white 400
■ deep red 435

THESE PILLOWS ARE WONDERFULLY CHUNKY. THE INSPIRATION
CAME FROM TRADITIONAL NORWEGIAN KNITTING PATTERNS.

HOME IS WHERE THE HEART IS

SETESDAL PILLOW

HEART MEASUREMENTS: Width 17¼in (44cm), height 22½in (57cm).

MATERIALS:
• Wadding

YARN: Dale Hegre (100% wool, 50g = 82yd/75m), 500g charcoal 0083, 100g natural 0017, 50g red 3828, and 100g moss 8972.

NEEDLES: US 36 (20mm).

GAUGE: 5.5 sts x 7.5 rows with six strands of yarn held together = 4 x 4in (10 x 10cm).

♥ ————————————————————————

Cast on with six strands of yarn held together and knit Regular heart (see p. 9). After increasing to 10 sts, knit color pattern following chart below.

Stuff the finished heart with wadding and sew up any gaps.

TEXTURED PILLOW

HEART MEASUREMENTS: Width 17¼in (44cm), height 22½in (57cm).

MATERIALS:

• Wadding

YARN: Dale Hegre (100% wool, 50g = 82yd/75m), 500g light gray 0004.

NEEDLES: US 36 (20mm).

GAUGE: 5.5 sts x 7.5 rows with six strands of yarn held together = 4 x 4in (10 x 10cm).

♥ ————————————————————————

Cast on with six strands of yarn held together and knit Regular heart (see p. 9). After increasing to 10 sts, knit stitch pattern following left-hand chart on p. 104.

Stuff the finished heart with wadding and sew up any gaps.

■ charcoal 0083
□ natural 0017
■ red 3828
■ moss 8972

All the pillows are knitted with six strands of yarn held together. If you don't have six balls of yarn in the same color, you can use three but knit from both ends. If you have fewer than three you will need to wind your own balls or buy more yarn.

GRAY AND WHITE PILLOW

HEART MEASUREMENTS: Width 17¼in (44cm), height 22½in (57cm).

MATERIALS:

• Wadding

YARN: Dale Hegre (100% wool, 50g = 82yd/75m), 350g gray 0083 and 250g natural 0017.

NEEDLES: US 36 (20mm).

GAUGE: 5.5 sts x 7.5 rows with six strands of yarn held together = 4 x 4in (10 x 10cm).

♥ ─────────────────────────────

Cast on with six strands of yarn held together and knit Regular heart (see p. 9). After increasing to 10 sts, knit color pattern following right-hand chart below.

Stuff the finished heart with wadding and sew up any gaps.

Heart's choice

Alexandra (stylist):
My favorites are these large pillows made in classical Norwegian patterns. They create nostalgia for Norway and Norwegian traditions: winter and snow, pasture and cabin. Comfort...

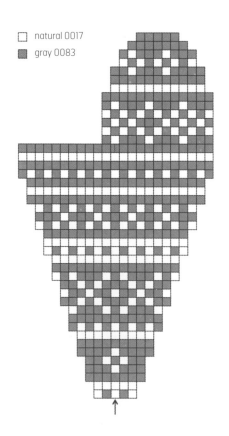

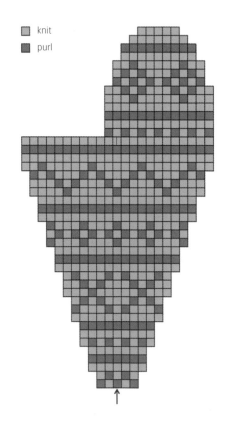

☐ knit
■ purl

☐ natural 0017
■ gray 0083

ANGEL HEARTS

WHITE ANGEL HEART

HEART MEASUREMENTS: Width 4¼in (11cm), height 5in (12.5cm).

MATERIALS:
- Wadding
- Glossy print
- White down
- White ribbon for hanging
- Matte enamel or decoupage glue (optional)
- Glue

YARN: Fine wool (100% wool, 50g = 191yd/175m) 50g white 400; Plum (70% mohair, 30% polyamide, 25g = 273yd/250m), leftovers or 25g white 001.

NEEDLES: US 4 (3.5mm).

GAUGE: 22 sts x 35 rows with one strand of each yarn = 4 x 4in (10 x 10cm).

♥ ————————————————————————

HEART: Cast on with one strand of each yarn and knit Regular heart (see p. 9).

Stuff the finished heart with wadding and sew up any gaps.

EMBELLISHMENTS: Glue the glossy print onto the heart. Paint it with enamel if desired to make it last longer.

TO FINISH: Attach ribbon and down between the curves of the heart.

BLUE-GREEN ANGEL HEART

HEART MEASUREMENTS: Width 4¼in (11cm), height 5in (12.5cm).

MATERIALS:
- Wadding
- Beads
- Glossy print
- Gray angel wings, 3in (8cm)
- White ribbon for hanging
- Matte enamel or decoupage glue (optional)
- Glue

YARN: Fine wool (100% wool, 50g = 191yd/175m) 50g light blue 4406; Plum (70% mohair, 30% polyamide, 25g = 273yd/250m), leftovers or 25g gray-green 058.

NEEDLES: US 4 (3.5mm).

GAUGE: 22 sts x 35 rows with one strand of each yarn = 4 x 4in (10 x 10cm).

♥ ————————————————————————

HEART: Cast on with one strand of each yarn and knit Regular heart (see p. 9).

Stuff the finished heart with wadding and sew up any gaps.

EMBELLISHMENTS: Attach beads evenly over the heart. Glue wings to the back. Glue the glossy print onto the heart. Paint it with enamel if desired to make it last longer.

TO FINISH: Attach ribbon between the curves of the heart.

The angels look good from both the front and back, so hang them where you can see both sides – on the Christmas tree, in a window, or maybe above your dining-room table.

Heart's choice

Anne Britt
(heart knitter)
These three are my favorites; they complement each other perfectly. Hearts, feathers, and vintage prints make me nostalgic. I think of my great-grandmother, who taught me how to knit.

GRAY ANGEL HEART

HEART MEASUREMENTS: Width 4¼in (11cm), height 5in (12.5cm).

MATERIALS:

- Wadding
- Glossy print
- White angel wings, 2½ x 3in (6.5 x 8cm)
- Light gray ribbon for hanging
- Matte enamel or decoupage glue (optional)
- Glue (glue gun)

YARN: Fine wool (100% wool, 50g = 191yd/175m), 50g blue-gray 4287; Plum (70% mohair, 30% polyamide, 25g = 273yd/250m), leftovers or 25g gray 057.

NEEDLES: US 4 (3.5mm).

GAUGE: 22 sts x 35 rows with one strand of each yarn = 4 x 4in (10 x 10cm).

♥ —————————————————————

HEART: Cast on with one strand of each yarn and knit Regular heart (see p. 9).

Stuff the finished heart with wadding and sew up any gaps.

EMBELLISHMENTS: Glue the wings to the back. Glue the glossy print onto the heart. Paint it with enamel if desired to make it last longer.

TO FINISH: Attach ribbon between the curves of the heart.

HERE WE CELEBRATE TYPICAL NORWEGIAN MOTIFS: MOOSE
IN THE SUNSET, EIGHT-LEAVED ROSE, AND HEARTS,
INSPIRED BY TRADITIONAL KNITTING PATTERNS.

WITH A HEART FOR TRADITION

FIVE HEARTS ON A WREATH

HEART MEASUREMENTS: Width 3½in (9cm),
height 4½in (11cm).

MATERIALS:
- Wadding
- Wreath

YARN: Ask HIFA 2 (100% wool, 100g = 344yd/315m),
leftovers or 50g in each of unbleached white 6057,
light brown mélange 6058, brown mélange 6102,
and dark brown mélange 6103.

NEEDLES: US ½ (2.5mm).

GAUGE: 27 st x 40 rows = 4 x 4in (10 x 10cm).

♥ ——————————————————————

HEARTS: Cast on using the top color from
the chart of your choice below and knit the
Regular heart (see p. 9). After increasing to
10 sts, knit the color patterns following the
charts below.

Stuff the finished heart with wadding and
sew up any gaps.

TO FINISH: Attach the five hearts to the
wreath – you can sew them, glue them, or
attach them with safety pins.

 If you use safety pins you can
take the hearts off the wreath
and put them elsewhere.

☐ unbleached white 6057
■ brown mélange 6102

⬚ light brown mélange 6058
■ brown mélange 6102

■ brown mélange 6102
☐ unbleached white 6057

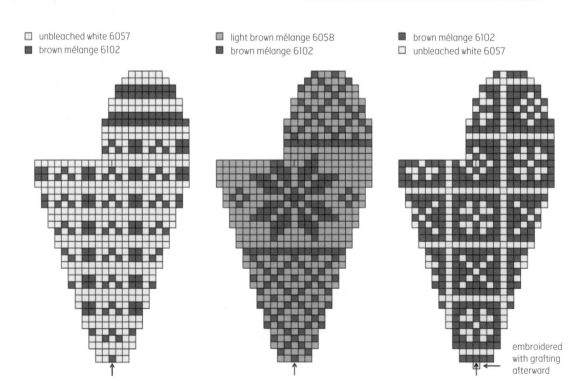

embroidered
with grafting
afterward

I chose to knit all the hearts in natural colors. I think this creates a pleasant atmosphere while at the same time being beautifully understated.

☐ unbleached white 6057
■ dark brown mélange 6103

■ dark brown mélange 6103
■ light brown mélange 6058

WELCOME HOME...

THREE DOOR HEARTS

HEART MEASUREMENTS: Width 3½in (9cm), height 5in (13cm).

MATERIALS:
• Wadding

YARN: Ask HIFA 2 (100% wool, 50g = 202yd/158m), leftovers or 50g of unbleached white 316057, light brown mélange 316058, and brown mélange 316102; leftovers in different colors for embroidery and hanging (optional).

NEEDLES: US ½ (2.5mm) plus C2/D3 (3mm) crochet hook.

Gauge: 27 sts x 40 rows = 4 x 4in (10 x 10cm).

♥ ————————————————————

Knit a heart in each of unbleached white, light brown mélange, and brown mélange yarn.

HEARTS: Cast on and knit Long heart (see p. 9).

Stuff the finished heart with wadding and sew up any gaps.

HANGING: Using the color of your choice, crochet a chain 10–13¾in (25–35cm) long. Turn and crochet 1 sl st in each ch. Fold the chain to form a loop, sew the edge together, and attach it to the pit of the heart.

EMBROIDERY: Embroider as desired, following the illustrations below for guidance.

knot stitch

straight stitch

outline stitch

The hearts look good with embroidered embellishments, but you could also leave them plain.

MERRY CHRISTMAS

HEART DECORATION

HEART MEASUREMENTS: Width 9½in (24cm), height 13in (33cm).

MATERIALS:

- 1 ball of thread in bleached natural
- Wadding
- "Merry Christmas" letters in zinc, height 4in (9.5cm)
- A dry branch, approx. 21¾in (55cm) long
- Glue (glue gun)
- Natural-colored string for hanging

YARN: Plum (70% mohair, 30% polyamide, 25g = 273yd/250m), leftovers or 25g white 001 or natural 003.

NEEDLES: US 13 (9mm), plus B1 (2mm) and E4 (3.5mm) crochet hooks.

GAUGE: 10 sts x 16 rows = 4 x 4in (10 x 10cm).

♥ ————————————————————————

HEART: Cast on with bleached natural thread and knit Regular heart (see p. 9).

Stuff the finished heart with wadding and sew up any gaps.

SMALL LEAVES: Use white or natural Plum yarn and B1 (2mm) crochet hook. Make 9 ch. Make a turning ch of 2 ch and crochet this in 9 ch:

1 dc in first ch, 1 tr in next ch, 2 dtr in next ch, 1 dtr in each of the next 4 ch, 2 dtr in next ch, then follow this in last st: 2 tr + 1 dtr + picot (= 2 ch, crochet 1 sl st in the first) +1 dtr + 2 tr. Cont on other side of loop with sts distributed like this: 2 dtr in next ch, 1 quad tr in each of the next 4 ch, 2 dtr in next ch, 1 tr in next l ch, 1 in last ch, 1 sl st at the edge of the leaf. Rep for desired number of leaves.

LARGE LEAVES: Use white or nature Plum yarn held double and E4 (3.5mm) hook. Crochet the desired number of leaves following pattern for Small leaves.

TO FINISH: Sew "Merry Christmas" letters onto the heart. Twist a string of natural-colored yarn and attach the heart to the branch. Use the same string to hang the decoration.

Glue leaves to the branch. Alternatively, use some glue where the string is attached to the branch to stabilize the position of the branch.

Heart's choice

Inger Margrethe
(editor)
It's very welcoming to be greeted by a heart, as they symbolize warmth and openness.

If you want the decoration to last for a long time, hang it inside rather than outdoors.

GOD JUL

Your own heart

HEART WORKSHOP

MAKE YOUR OWN...

Select the yarn you want to use.

Use needles a little smaller than what is suggested on the yarn label so the knitted fabric will be dense (presuming that you will fill it with wadding).

Create your own stitch or color patterns as you like, using the charts right for the Regular or Long hearts. Follow the pattern instructions set out on p. 9. After increasing to 10 sts, knit the stitch or color pattern from your chart.

Fill the finished heart with wadding, if desired, and sew up any gaps.

 ────────────────────

NOTE:

- In the pattern and chart the front and back of the heart has an odd number of stitches. If you want a pattern based off-center you will need to work with an odd number of stitches.

- If you want to use several colors in the design it can be a good idea not to make them too far apart on the wrong side. (If you're embroidering the design onto the heart you don't need to worry about this.)

- The heart charts are made with almost "square" squares. In real life, the stitches will be wider than they are tall. This means that your pattern will be flattened when knitted — how much depends on the yarn.

- Try to knit a relatively tight gauge for the yarn so you avoid having the wadding show through the knitted stitches.

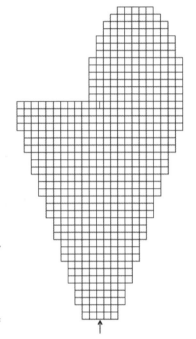

Regular heart

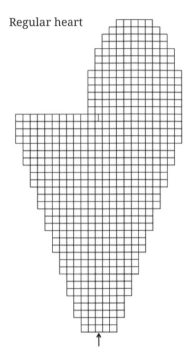

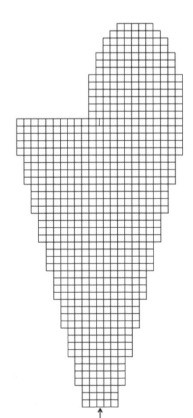

Long heart

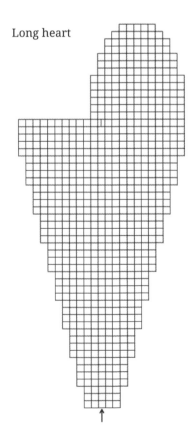

USEFUL INFORMATION

US AND METRIC SIZES

The American system of sizing knitting needles and crochet hooks is different from the metric system, where the diameter of needles and hooks is simply measured in millimeters. Sometimes there are not exact equivalents between the two systems. If this is the case with a design you would like to make, just choose the closest available size of needle or hook. It will also be particularly important to check your gauge!

AMERICAN AND EUROPEAN KNITTING AND CROCHET TERMS

Just in case you weren't confused enough already, sometimes stitches and technical terms are called different things in the US and in Europe. Here's a quick guide.

KNITTING TERMS

US terms	European terms
bind off	cast off
gauge	tension
seed stitch	moss stitch
stockinette stitch (st st)	stocking stitch (st st)

CROCHET TERMS

US terms	European terms
single crochet (sc)	double crochet (dc)
half double crochet (hdc)	half treble (htr)
double crochet (dc)	treble (tr)
treble (tr)	double treble (dtr)
double treble (dtr)	triple treble (ttr)
triple treble (ttr)	quadruple treble (quadtr)
quadruple treble (quadtr)	quintuple treble (quintr)

KNITTING NEEDLE SIZES

US size	Metric size
0	2mm
1	2.25mm
–	2.5mm
2	2.75mm
–	3mm
3	3.25mm
4	3.5mm
5	3.75mm
6	4mm
7	4.5mm
8	5mm
9	5.5mm
10	6mm
10 ½	6.5mm
–	7mm
–	7.5mm
11	8mm
13	9mm
15	10mm
17	12mm
19	15mm
36	20mm

CROCHET HOOK SIZES

US sizes	Metric sizes
B1	2.25mm
–	2.5mm
C2	2.75mm
–	3mm
D3	3.25mm
E4	3.5mm
F5	3.75mm
G6	4mm
7	4.5mm
H8	5mm
I9	5.5mm
J10	6mm
K10½	6.5mm
–	7mm
L11	8mm
M/N13	9mm
N/P15	10mm
O16	12mm

BENTE'S LITTLE KNITTING CLASS

CASTING ON

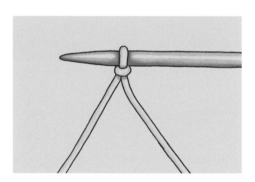

1. Make a loop in the yarn as shown.

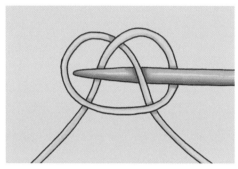

2. Tighten the loop around the needle.

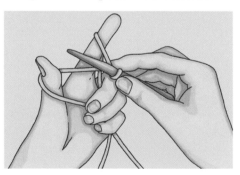

3. Hold the needle in your right hand and the yarn in your left hand, as shown. It doesn't matter what end of the yarn you use.

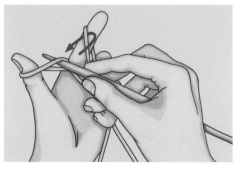

4. Insert the needle under the yarn that is in front of the left-hand thumb. Make the needle go over and behind the yarn on the left thumb, following the arrow...

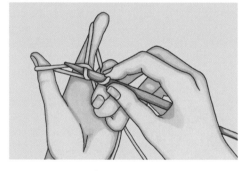

5. ... and pull the needle back the same way.

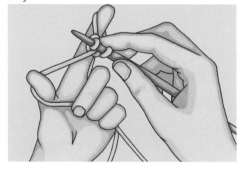

6. Remove the thumb from the loop and tighten. You have now made one stitch, so there are two stitches on the needle (including the original loop). Continue to cast on by repeating steps 4–6, until you have the desired number of stitches.

THE KNIT STITCH

1. Insert right needle through first stitch on left needle from left side of loop.

2. Wind the yarn around the needle as per the arrow in illustration 1, and pull it back through the stitch. The new loop now forms a knit stitch on the right needle.

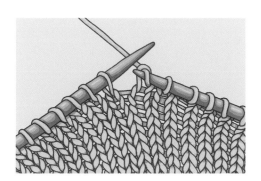

3. Release the old stitch from the left needle.

THE PURL STITCH

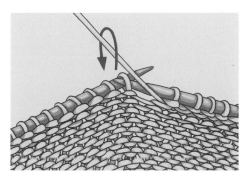

1. Insert right needle through first stitch on left needle, from the right side of the loop.

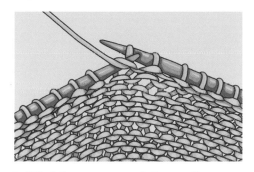

2. Wind the yarn around the needle as per the arrow in illustration 1, and pull it back through the stitch. The new loop forms a purl stitch on the right needle.

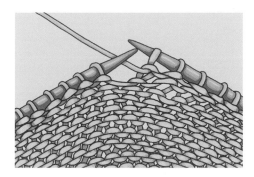

3. Release the old stitch from the left needle.

DECREASE 1 STITCH BY KNITTING TWO TOGETHER

1. Work as if making a regular knit stitch, but insert the needle through the first two stitches on the left needle and knit together.

BIND OFF

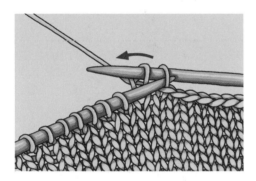

1. Knit two stitches, then pull the first over the second, as per the arrow above. You have now bound off one stitch and there is one stitch on right needle.

To bind off another stitch, knit one more stitch and pull the old stitch from the right needle over the new one. Repeat until the desired number of stitches have been bound off.

If every stitch is to be bound off, repeat until there is one stitch remaining on the right needle. Cut the yarn and pull right needle with the stitch on it until the end of the yarn and the stitch comes out. Pull the yarn tight and tie off.

ABBREVIATIONS

KNITTING

approx.	approximately
beg	beginning
cm	centimeter(s)
cont	continue
dec	decrease/decreasing
g	gram(s)
in	inch(es)
inc	increase/increasing
k	knit
k2tog	knit two stitches together (decrease by one stitch)
kwise	knitwise
m	meter(s)
oz	ounce(s)
p	purl
patt	pattern
psso	pass the slipped stitch over
rem	remain/ing
rep	repeat
RS	right side
sl	slip
st(s)	stitch(es)
st st	stockinette stitch
tog	together
WS	wrong side
yd	yard(s)
*	repeat directions following * as many times as indicated

CROCHET

ch	chain
dc	double crochet
dtr	double treble
quad tr	quadruple treble
sc	single crochet
sl st	slip stitch
st(s)	stitch(es)
tog	together
tr	treble

SUPPLIERS

UK

ARTESANO
www.artesanoyarns.co.uk
Unit G, Lamb's Farm Business Park
Basingstoke Road
Swallowfield
Reading
RG7 1PQ
Tel: +44 (0)118 950 3350

BRAMWELL CRAFTS
www.bramwellcrafts.co.uk
Campbell Road
Stoke-on-Trent
Staffordshire
ST4 4ET
Tel: +44 (0)1782 745000

COATS CRAFTS
www.coatscrafts.co.uk
PO Box 22
Lingfield House
Lingfield Point
McMullen Road
Darlington
DL1 1YJ
Tel: +44 (0)1325 394237

CYGNET YARNS
www.cygnetyarns.com
12-14 Adelaide Street
Bradford
West Yorkshire
BD5 0EF
Tel: +44 (0)1274 743374

ROWAN
www.knitrowan.com
Green Lane Mill
Holmfirth
West Yorkshire
England
HD9 2DX
Tel: +44 (0)1484 681881

SIRDAR
www.sirdar.co.uk
Flanshaw Lane
Alvethorpe
Wakefield
WF2 9ND
Tel: +44 (0)1924 371501

STITCH CRAFT CREATE
www.stitchcraftcreate.co.uk
Brunel House
Forde Close
Newton Abbot
Devon
TQ12 4PU
Tel +44 (0)1626 323219

TWILLEYS
www.twilleys.co.uk
Twilleys of Stamford
Roman Mill
Stamford
PE9 1BG
Tel: +44 (0)1780 752661

USA / CANADA

KNITTING FEVER
www.knittingfever.com
315 Bayview Avenue
Amityville, NY 11701
USA
Tel: +1 516 546 3600

PATONS YARNS
www.patonsyarns.com
320 Livingstone Avenue South
Listowel
Ontario, N4W 3H3
Canada
Tel: +1 888 368 8401

WESTMINSTER FIBERS
www.westminsterfibers.com
165 Ledge Street
Nashua, NH 03060
USA
Tel: +1 603 886 5041/5043

AUSTRALIA

AUSTRALIAN COUNTRY SPINNERS
www.auspinners.com.au
Level 7, 409 St Kilda Road
Melbourne
Victoria 3004
Tel: +61 (0)3 9380 3888

CREATIVE IMAGES
PO Box 106
Hastings
Victoria 3915
Tel: +61 (0)3 5979 1555

I love coffee

TEMPLATES

All templates are shown at actual size, unless otherwise stated.

Enlarge by 200%

the way to the heart...

index

A DAVID & CHARLES BOOK
© Cappelen Damm AS 2012

Originally published in Norway as *Med Hjerte For Strikk*
First published in the UK and USA in 2013 by F&W Media International, Ltd

David & Charles is an imprint of F&W Media International, Ltd
Brunel House, Forde Close, Newton Abbot, TQ12 4PU, UK

F&W Media International, Ltd is a subsidiary of F+W Media, Inc
10151 Carver Road, Suite #200, Blue Ash, OH 45242, USA

Bente Presterud Røvik has asserted her right to be identified as author of this work in accordance with the Copyright, Designs and Patents Act, 1988.

A catalogue record for this book is available from the British Library.

ISBN-13: 978-1-4463-0321-4 paperback
ISBN-10: 1-4463-0321-7 paperback

Printed in China by RR Donnelley for F&W Media International, Ltd
Brunel House, Forde Close, Newton Abbot, TQ12 4PU, UK

10 9 8 7 6 5 4 3 2 1

Photographer: Guri Pheifer
Stylist: Alexandra Villefrance
Book design: Laila Gundersen

F+W Media publishes high quality books on a wide range of subjects. For more great book ideas visit:
www.stitchcraftcreate.co.uk